Praise for *The Magic of Surrender*

"Simply amazing. *The Magic of Surrender* is heartfelt, inspiring, and catapults you into a new life. By using the principles Kute teaches, you will be able to create a truly miraculous life. Get ready for your life to shift."

—**Marci Shimoff**, *New York Times*–bestselling author of *Happy for No Reason*

"Kute's book *The Magic of Surrender* is a much-needed powerful resource filled with emotional and spiritual tools for discovering freedom and peace within one's self. A resource for navigating through a world where our trust gets broken, and we can become easily lost in indecision and fear and feel as if we don't have control. So many lose sight on their path and journey and struggle with their purpose. This is a life-changing guide about the importance of surrendering, facing our truth, and finding our true calling and purpose."

—**Anthony William**, **#1** *New York Times*–bestselling author of the **Medical Medium series**

"In *The Magic of Surrender*, Kute Blackson offers his depth of experience and wise words to illuminate the experience of surrender. With his guidance, you will discover how you can surrender to life's challenges in ways that create resilience and buoyancy."

—**Arielle Ford**, author of *The Soulmate Secret*

"Kute's new book touches on some of the deepest life lessons each of us must face. The profoundly spiritual topics of surrender and letting go were made easily relatable and relevant because they were brought to us with Kute's trademark humble and yet brilliant sense of humor. You feel empowered as if each chapter hands you a piece of magic that transforms the foundation of your life. This is practical spirituality made easy."

—**Ken Honda**, bestselling author of *Happy Money*

"*The Magic of Surrender* shows you the pathway to true freedom. When you are ready to create a life beyond your wildest imagination and manifest your face off, Kute Blackson demystifies the concept of surrender and shows you how in his unique and loving way."

—**Emily Fletcher**, founder of **Ziva Meditation**

"*The Magic of Surrender* is a unique book filled with life-changing wisdom. It will challenge you beyond your limitations and help you tap into your infinite potential. Not your typical self-help book."

—John Gray, bestselling relationship author of
Men Are from Mars, Women Are from Venus

"*The Magic of Surrender* is a life-changing book filled with practical wisdom and powerful stories. Kute Blackson teaches you step by step how to surrender and to open to your soul's guidance."

—Dr. John Demartini, internationally bestselling author of
The Values Factor and *The Breakthrough Experience*

"*The Magic of Surrender* will shift your energy and catapult you to the next level in your life. Kute Blackson boldly invites you to live a life bigger than you can imagine. One of the best books you will read. Thank you, Kute!"

—Dr. Sue Morter, author of the #1 bestselling book *The Energy Codes*, founder of Morter Institute for BioEnergetics, and creator of BodyAwake Yoga

"Kute Blackson is a leading visionary in the field of personal development. His work is remarkable, powerful, and will transform your life."

—Larry King, Emmy– and Peabody Award–winning
talk show host

"*The Magic of Surrender* is a powerful book to help you navigate the challenging time we are in. This book will guide you beyond what you thought possible for your life, help you access you own greatness, and fulfill your destiny. Kute Blackson is a leader for the new generation."

—Jack Canfield, coauthor of *The Success Principles* and
the #1 *New York Times*–bestselling Chicken Soup for
the Soul series™

"This powerful book will remind you about what really matters, and guide you back to living your deepest truth. Kute Blackson shows you that living aligned with your heart is the most powerful way to manifest the life you truly desire. The pages of *The Magic of Surrender* are filled with inspiration!"

—Tara Brach, author of *Radical Acceptance* and
Radical Compassion

"At a time when so many of us are struggling to find solutions to personal and global problems, Kute Blackson teaches us how to solve those problems—without struggling. When Blackson tells us surrender ushers us into magic, he's not parroting New Age slogans; his advice rings with authenticity, wisdom, and truth. *The Magic of Surrender* is a brilliant guide and companion that takes us not only past our difficulties but straight into a benevolent mystery. Read it as a treat for your soul."

—**Martha Beck,** *New York Times*–**bestselling author of** *Finding Your Own North Star*

"A mesmerizing account of finding the courage to let go and trust the Universe, only to find your life guided with extraordinary precision. Filled with tips on how anyone can do the same, Kute Blackson is a modern-day mystic with a gift for showing others the way to their purpose and passions."

—**Mike Dooley,** *New York Times*–**bestselling author of** *Infinite Possibilities*

"*The Magic of Surrender* will inspire your soul to its highest potential. Kute Blackson will help you create magic in your life. Read this book cover to cover, take action, and watch miracles happen for you!"

—**Les Brown,** *New York Times*–**bestselling author of** *Live Your Dreams*

"There are many moments on our soul journey that require a surrender and an offering up of what we've been holding onto. Surrender isn't meant to break us down—it's meant to break us open. In *The Magic of Surrender*, Kute Blackson offers a personal and inspiring guide to finding more freedom and peace by understanding the amazing spiritual power of surrender."

—**Dr. Barbara De Angelis, #1** *New York Times*–**bestselling author of** *Soul Shifts*

The
MAGIC of
SURRENDER

Finding the Courage
to Let Go

KUTE BLACKSON

A TarcherPerigee Book

TarcherPerigee

An imprint of Penguin Random House LLC

penguinrandomhouse.com

Most TarcherPerigee books are available at special quantity discounts for bulk purchase for sales promotions, premiums, fund-raising, and educational needs. Special books or book excerpts also can be created to fit specific needs. For details, write: SpecialMarkets@penguinrandomhouse.com.

Library of Congress Cataloging-in-Publication Data

Names: Blackson, Kute, author.
Title: The magic of surrender / Kute Blackson.
Description: New York: TarcherPerigee, Penguin Random House LLC, 2021.
Identifiers: LCCN 2020041095 (print) | LCCN 2020041096 (ebook) |
ISBN 9780593189092 (hardcover) | ISBN 9780593189108 (ebook)
Subjects: LCSH: Self-actualization (Psychology). |
Self-realization. | Conduct of life.
Classification: LCC BF637.S4 B557 2021 (print) |
LCC BF637.S4 (ebook) | DDC 158.1—dc23
LC record available at https://lccn.loc.gov/2020041095
LC ebook record available at https://lccn.loc.gov/2020041096

Printed in the United States of America
1st Printing

Book design by Patrice Sheridan

For my mother.
You taught me the real meaning of surrender.
And your spirit lives on in my heart.

CONTENTS

PROLOGUE

WHEN THE RING of my phone awakened me, I glanced out the window. The sun was not yet up.

Deep in the pit of my stomach, I knew something was wrong.

As my eyes came into focus, I glanced at the screen. It was my father.

In my half-awake state, I fumbled to answer it, but before I could, it went to voicemail. I took a few deep breaths, and then listened to the message that he had just recorded.

"Kute, it's your father. I need to speak to you."

I rubbed my eyes and tried to wake myself as I called my father back. "Dad. What's going on?"

I waited as the words traveled across the miles from Ghana to Los Angeles.

"Kute, I'm sorry, but I just got a phone call from your mother. It turns out, she has cancer."

I tried to breathe, but it was like I had forgotten how. I felt like a statue. Was my heart still beating? I couldn't tell. But if I didn't move, maybe it wouldn't be real.

Finally, I heard my father saying my name, his voice insistent and impatient. Waiting for me to answer.

"I'm sorry, Dad. I'm here."

"I need you to go to London."

"Of course, I'll get on the next flight."

I hung up and called my mother, my heart beating frantically, as if it wanted to make up for those beats it had missed while I processed the news.

"Mom? I just got a call from Dad. What's going on?"

I tried to keep my voice steady, but I felt shaken to my core. My mother's calm voice came through as if she were in the room with me. "I went in for some tests last week. I didn't want to worry you. It's okay. There is nothing to do until they run a few more tests. Then we will know how the doctors plan to treat it. Don't worry, it is okay. I'm okay."

We spoke for a few more minutes and she promised me she'd call after the next round of tests.

I was in a daze for the rest of the day.

This was just like my mother, to downplay something serious. Nothing ever rattled her. She always trusted that God had everything under control. She had a level of faith that I'd always found truly unbelievable.

I like to say that I was born from this faith. My mother, a Japanese woman, agreed to marry my father, a healer from Ghana, before she had even met him. She was twenty-eight, considered an old maid in the eyes of her Japanese society. Though those around her worried about her prospects, she had faith, and prayed daily that God would lead her to her husband. One day, she heard that a miracle man from Africa would be coming to visit the spiritual organization she was a part of. She immediately felt deep in her soul a knowing. *This man will be your husband.* She sent him a letter, with help from her sister, who spoke English.

When my father received the letter, he had a knowing as well. *This is my wife.* He wrote back, and asked whether she might be willing to move to Ghana.

"If it's God's will," she wrote, in her second letter to him.

My father wrote again and asked her to marry him.

And she said yes.

My parents did not speak a common language. They had never met when they agreed to be married. Didn't even know what the other looked like. The first time they saw each other they had to communicate using dictionaries (which they did for years afterward).

It takes an intense level of faith to live your life that way.

And yet that was how my mother lived her life every single day.

My mother said there was no reason for me to come to London until her first treatment. So I stayed in touch with her daily, until a few weeks later, when I flew from L.A. to accompany her to her first appointment. When I arrived from the airport, I burst into her apartment and wrapped her in my arms. She still looked well. She still bantered with me like she always did. And as we headed to her appointment, her spirits were high.

"I'm ready for whatever God has in store for me. I'm at peace."

Just like her prayer for her soul mate, she had no conditions on what would happen. She was open, and trusting. In love. In life. Surrendered.

And now, even facing death.

We arrived at the clinic and she got hooked up to an IV that would transfer what we hoped would be life-saving chemicals into her body for eight hours. We sat and talked about nothing and everything, laughing and joking like old times. And as I sat there, soaking up her presence, I realized that it had been years since we had sat together, with no agenda, nowhere to go, nowhere else to be. By the time the nurse came over to extract the IV, saying that the session was over, we looked at each other and laughed, both thinking the exact same thing: *Over already? I wish we had more time!*

I flew back for each of her chemo sessions, spaced a few weeks apart. Sometimes my mother would fall asleep for an hour or so, and I would just look at her. Truly look at her in a way that I never had before. She had lived such an unusual and beautiful life. To go from everything she knew in Japan to living in Ghana, married to a man she barely knew, then giving birth to a mixed-race baby, all while not being able to speak the native language. Yet she grew in faith at each new phase that she faced. And here she was, starting one more chapter that would have more lessons for her.

When she woke up, she looked at me gazing at her.

She could tell that, while I treasured this time we were spending together, I was sad. I wasn't ready to lose my mother. She took my hand in hers.

"Kute, this is just another opportunity for my soul's growth. I'm not the body, anyway. This is just a temporary vehicle for my spirit. This body is not who I really am. So if it is time to shed this form, I am ready."

Maybe she was ready, but I still wanted her by my side. I still had so much of my life that I wanted her to witness. Marriage one day, children. There were so many experiences that I would have that she would miss if she died now. I just wanted more. More of her. More time. And it didn't seem fair.

But as I spent time with my mother, I had to surrender to the fact that these were likely some of our last days. I knew that she was dying. I could no longer resist the truth. And because of that, I could truly see the beauty in front of me, even as I embraced the sadness that I was losing her.

As we took short walks, as we sat and talked about nothing and everything, as we worked together making sushi, cutting the cucumbers, and stirring the rice, my soul was taking it all in.

This is a miracle, this time together. Every single moment.

After three months of chemo treatments, there was no improvement. For a time, the doctors thought they might perform surgery, but after yet another round of tests revealed that the cancer had progressed too much, they determined the surgery would no longer do any good.

We had reached the end of our treatment options. Now, it was just about making her comfortable during her final days.

When I asked how much time she had left, her doctor said, "We aren't talking years. We are talking months, maybe weeks."

My mother nodded her head stoically, as I felt like my heart was breaking into a million pieces.

We walked out to the car, and I got my mother comfortably settled in the passenger seat before I got in to drive.

But I couldn't even start the engine. I looked over at my mother.

"Are you afraid of dying?"

She reached over and squeezed my hand gently. With a soft smile on her lips, she said: "Not at all. The soul lives forever. I am ready for whatever God wants for my life."

She was not lying.

This little Japanese lady was fearless.

She walked out of that doctor's office just as peaceful as she had been before. Dying, or not dying, she was surrendered. She knew that the body that held her spirit was not really who she truly was. She would continue to exist, even as she took her last breath. Yes, her existence would change, but it would not end.

I wished that I had access to that peace. Instead, I drove her home in a trance.

That night, I held her, sobbing. But even in my sadness, I felt grateful. I felt this deep sense of privilege that I knew her as a soul. That through each stage of my life, she had been guiding me, watching me, molding me into the person that I had become. She was amazing. A truly special human being. And I felt like I was realizing it for the very first time.

After my tears had dried, she pulled back and looked me in the eyes.

"Kute, none of us has control in this life. Our demand that life go the way we want is what causes so much suffering. Know that the degree to which you surrender determines the degree to which you are alive, the degree to which life can use you, the degree to which you can enjoy life," she said with a smile.

She took my hand, her eyes bright as ever, warm and filled with overwhelming love. "I will be watching over you and supporting you from the other side, cheering you on, always. Even during the moments when it is most difficult to trust, know that you are not alone, and that surrender is always worth it. It is the way. It is the key. It is the real secret."

LETTING GO

We began to make plans to fly her back to Ghana, where my father was living, and where she would spend her last days. She arrived in July, and as autumn descended, my father insisted she was doing well, but I knew each time I visited: death was drawing near. She was not as responsive as the visit before. Soon parts of her body were swollen in a way that signaled she did not have much time left.

One night, I sat at her bedside as she slept. I held her hand, trying to get in touch with the essence of who she was, with the part of her that would continue on even as her earthly physical body shut down.

I slowly placed my hand over my mother's heart and felt it beating. I closed my eyes and felt deep in my soul:

Listen to her heart. Feel it beating. That force, the energy behind the beating, is what she really is. It will never die. That essence will always live. Remember, even when you feel you've lost her, you can never lose her.

I knew that I needed to believe, like she did, that even without this body, without this form, my mother would still exist. Still be. Still love me, somewhere, somehow.

Knowing this deep in my bones, I was able to let her go. I whispered in her ear: "It's okay. I'm going to be fine. I release you and let you go."

Tears began to roll down my cheeks as I said: "I set you free."

I fell asleep that night, with my head on her bed, my forehead touching the warmth of her skin.

When she woke the next morning, she was in good spirits. I was scheduled to leave the following day. I didn't know whether I should go. But death is not something you can forecast. It is impossible to know the timing. So I flew back to L.A. as planned and had just landed when my cousin called.

"Your mother took a turn for the worse. She's not

responding at all. She's just chanting one word like a mantra, over and over. We can't figure out what it is." I tried to decipher it over the phone and speak to her, with no luck. The next day, a Monday, my cousin called again and she seemed better. I settled into the start of my week, and knew that I would fly back to Ghana as soon as I could.

Tuesday morning came, and I got up and went to my neighborhood juice bar. And as I stood in line, I noticed a song playing in the background.

Every breath you take, and every move you make, every bond you break, every step you take, I'll be watching you.

It was a very familiar song by The Police, and yet I knew it was not a random occurrence but a message from my mom. She was echoing those words she had spoken to me weeks ago: I'm going to be helping you fulfill your mission from the other side.

In my heart, did I know? That this was a sign? That she was preparing to leave? I don't know. I went to sleep that night like any other night. But I woke up in the middle of the night yet again. A phone call from my father.

My mother had passed away.

Two years have gone by since she left us. I miss her

every day. Yet despite the pain and sadness, I know that my mother's death was also a gift. It set me on a new mission.

My mother, through her life and through her death, showed me, firsthand, what it means to live the magic of surrender.

Everything that happened to her, the good, the bad, the hard and the easy, the beautiful, and the ugly, she embraced it and looked for the opportunity within it. She did not fight life, but trusted it fully. She somehow knew that even the hard times would give birth to something beautiful.

She lived with peacefulness and power. She lived surrendered and available.

She knew what it meant to be great.

And her example can be a guide for us all.

INTRODUCTION

WHAT IF THERE was one belief that could enhance every experience of your life?

One idea that could help you move through the stresses of life so you could face the day fully with an open heart?

One concept that could help you dream bigger, and truly step into more of your greatness than you could ever have imagined?

One principle that would allow you to enjoy your kids more, love your spouse fully, and savor the everyday moments?

And what if this was something you thought you needed to avoid at all costs?

I'm here to show you a different way. To introduce you to a way of life that has changed my life and holds the power to transform yours.

It's time to get real.

Many of us find ourselves stuck in an existence that is a fraction of what we truly desire. It's not your fault. It isn't for lack of trying. We are a generation of strivers. We dream and we do and we hustle.

But all that striving sometimes creates struggle. All that effort often leads to exhaustion.

Trust me, I've been there.

I'm here to suggest there is a different way.

I call it *the magic of surrender.*

We've been taught that surrender is weak.

But this is a misconception.

Surrender is the most powerful thing you can do.

We've been told that surrender is passive. That surrender means giving up, waving the white flag, and laying down our weapons.

We fear that if we surrender, we won't get what we desire. We're afraid that if we surrender, someone else will take what is ours. We'll lose. We'll be left behind.

In reality: What if you got so much more?

Surrender is the invitation to take all limits off of life

itself. So magic can happen. More than you can imagine. More than you could ever plan. More than you are able to fathom.

This is the magic.

But in order to access it, we must change the way we view surrender. So we can access its power and road map to freedom.

REDEFINED

Webster's Dictionary doesn't necessarily help. It defines surrender as this:

> *Surrender (v):*
> 1) to cease resistance to an enemy and submit to their authority.

But if you keep reading, down in the fourth entry, you discover these remarkable words:

> 4) To abandon oneself entirely (to an emotion or influence); give in to.

This is what I'm talking about. This is the concept of

surrender that can change your life. This is the surrender that is exciting, exhilarating, and freeing. This is the surrender that takes you beyond yourself, gets you out of the way, so that you can tap into and live the true greatness that is inside of you.

Beyond your past. Beyond your conditioning. Beyond your stories. Beyond what you previously thought was possible.

This surrender gives you access to a whole new level of possibilities for your life.

The blissful release you feel in the moment of orgasm?

It requires surrender.

The adrenaline that rushes when you jump out of a plane in a free fall as you abandon yourself to the pull of gravity?

It requires surrender.

To experience it, you have to let go.

The ecstasy that arises as you dance in a group of people, your individual moves lost in the crowd as you become one being, one surge of energy?

It requires surrender.

You must dissolve into the pack.

Let me make it clear.

Surrender isn't giving up.

It is tapping in. To a source that is bigger than your own personal power.

We often think letting go means you lose.

But what if letting go leads to more?

More joy. More power. More peace. More freedom. More love. More miracles. More of who you are. More of who you are meant to be. **And more than you could ever have imagined.**

Surrender is what happens when you take all the conditions off of life and stop trying to control everything. It's only then that you get everything. And the everything is more than you could have planned for yourself.

And there lies the paradox.

Imagine you boarded an airplane, ready to travel to an exotic destination.

But instead of finding your assigned seat on the plane and getting settled, letting the flight attendants bring you drinks, and turning on your personal TV, you made your way to the cockpit and began pounding on the door. You stood there, demanding to get in, to have access to the controls of the plane.

You are not a pilot. You have no idea how to fly that three-ton steel machine. But you wanted to make sure that you got where you wanted to go. So you tried to hijack the plane, for all twelve hours of your flight, instead of sitting back, having a snack, taking a nap, and trusting that the pilot would get you there.

It sounds like hell, doesn't it?

But that's how we live our lives. Convinced that we should be in control, pounding down the doors of the cockpit when things aren't going exactly according to our plan.

We protest, "Things weren't supposed to turn out this way!" And so we vehemently hold on to the way we thought life should have been, forcing our ideas that clearly weren't working instead of opening to the life that is actually seeking to happen.

And holding on to what isn't working simply holds us back from enjoying the amazing adventure that is our life.

DISCOVERING THE KEY

Today, I know the formula to my mother's freedom.

Surrender + Trust = MAGIC

Control + Resistance = SUFFERING

My guess is you might be well versed in the suffering.

So can you consider that today is a chance to try another way?

This is not some esoteric book of new age teaching, sharing impractical, unrelatable theories of surrender. It's a modern-day manual on how to surrender for real, and this kind of surrender gets results. You may think that surrender is just for the spiritual ones. But no. Surrender can be lived in everyday life.

We often surrender as a last resort. I'm actually inviting you to surrender as a first resort, as the first option, as the very foundation of your life.

So whether you have a family member facing addiction, or you were diagnosed with a supposedly incurable disease, or you've been trying to get pregnant with a child for years, or you are single and you desperately long for your soul mate, or you just got fired from your job, or you are dealing with a toxic family member, all of these situations require surrender. Even if you were to surrender just five or ten percent more today, and be more open to what life wants to give you, I assure you, you would feel lighter, more powerful, more grounded.

But surrender does more than just help you face your problems head on. It does more than improve your enjoyment of life.

It allows you to go from living a good life to living a great life.

A life of impact.

A life of importance.

A life of legacy.

It is the unspoken key to all the great ones throughout history.

Consider Muhammad Ali. He had a successful life as an athlete. But when he was vilified for his resistance to the Vietnam conflict, for his refusal to fight in a war he did not believe in, he stood firm in his convictions, surrendered his success, sacrificed his title, his livelihood, and his safety, and, in the end, his actions would inspire generations and become his legacy. He became more than a boxer and instead an icon of integrity.

This is surrender.

Or think about Malala Yousafzai, who put herself in harm's way because of her desire for an education. She did not allow the tragedy that unfolded to silence her but allowed it to propel her forward. She became a voice of hope for young women worldwide. She surrendered her small life, and now travels the world as an example of resilience.

This is surrender.

Or consider Viktor Frankl. A man who refused to give in to despair in the concentration camps, who did not give up when all his family members perished, but survived and was determined to find meaning even in the most hopeless of situations. And once free, he committed his life to helping others discover the meaning that he knew saved his own life.

This is surrender.

Surrender is Colin Kaepernick taking a knee, sacrificing the career he'd worked so hard for to stand for something much bigger than a ball. His actions became prophetic, a symbol for speaking up without words. Whether you agree with his actions or not, you have to respect an individual who is putting his money where his mouth is and surrendering to his soul's calling. What he is doing is bigger than politics. He felt something, and he went with it. It cost him his career.

But in the end, he will be remembered for so much more than a few touchdowns and a Super Bowl.

This is surrender.

Surrender is Sojourner Truth, a slave who walked away from her chains, had the bravery to sue for ownership of her son, and spent her life fighting for the rights of people like her. Despite the fact she could not read or write, she knew her voice had worth and wasn't afraid to speak up. She was committed to proving that women deserved to have the same rights as men, and gave her life to securing equal footing for all people.

This is surrender.

People think surrender is weak, that it means you allow yourself to be taken advantage of, or that it requires lighting incense, chanting mantras, simply saying *namaste*.

No. Surrender is powerful.

To surrender is to give up trying to force life into what you think it should be and be willing to embrace the unknown—and be open to what is seeking to happen.

To surrender is to not compromise who you are, to have the courage to be disliked, and to take a stand for what you know is right.

To surrender is to dare to love fully despite the risks.

This is when the magic unfolds.

We must let go of what is good for what is great.

We must release what is mediocre for the magical.

We must be ready to shed what is superficial and what we are settling for to experience what is sincere.

So here's the secret.

If you want magic . . . you must surrender.

I'm going to show you how.

CHAPTER ONE

HOW TO GET OUT OF YOUR OWN WAY

EGO

THIS BOOK WILL give you access to magic.

No, I don't mean Harry Potter or Hocus Pocus. I'm talking about everyday magic that is available to us all, in each moment, every second. But everyday magic is no less amazing.

Magic takes you from ordinary to extraordinary. Magic transforms the seemingly mundane into the miraculous.

Magic is always available. But we're not always available to it.

Magic can only happen once we get ourselves out of the way.

Think about those whom you might consider great.

They are only great because they didn't let their small plans of what they thought their lives should be limit who they became.

Dr. Martin Luther King Jr. could have remained a local preacher. And stayed in the safe zone.

Mahatma Gandhi could have given up his fight for the untouchables and simply pursued prestige as a lawyer.

Mother Teresa could have stayed in the convent and been comfortable instead of going out to serve the sick and the poor.

But they chose to listen—not to ego, but to their souls. To an undeniable calling. They were open to life leading them, rather than trying to fit life into their little concept of what they thought it should be.

Something bigger, something that they could no longer resist, was seeking to happen in their lives.

When we stay focused only on what *we* want, we stay stuck in our limited desires, rather than opening to the big plans that life has for us. And while what we want may be good, what life wants is beyond good. Life has no limits. Remember, life is bigger than what you can imagine.

It's time to go beyond personal power.

This is when the magic unfolds.

STALKING FREEDOM

I stared out the window of the crowded train.

I had been traveling for over thirty hours. I had four more to go.

The dry countryside transformed before my eyes into a land that was lush, green, and tropical. Though I was still in India, it didn't feel like it. It looked like paradise. I longed to get off the train and breathe the fresh air that called to me just past the dusty windowpane.

I was on my way to Kerala, in the southwest portion of India, on the shores of the Arabian Sea. Once there, I was supposed to find a man named Gangoli. He sounded like an Italian mafia boss, but people said he was an enlightened being. I didn't know what that meant. But I was curious to find out.

I was twenty-four years old and on a quest for answers. My life hadn't turned out the way I had expected. I was in search of some insight into why I was not where I thought I was supposed to be.

When I moved to America at eighteen, I had nothing. No money. No contacts. No plan.

But I had a head and heart full of determination and hope, to chase the American dream.

Everyone in my life had assumed that I would stay in London and take over my father's legacy, three hundred churches spread throughout Africa and London. It was what I had been groomed to do since the age of eight, when he called me up to the pulpit to give my first sermon. He was a renowned preacher, famous for his healing powers, a man who spoke powerfully and transformed people's lives.

I had the speaking gift as well. I had always dreamed of speaking in front of crowds, like my father. But I didn't want to stay in London. I didn't want to teach and inspire and heal the way my father did. I wanted to forge my own path. Take the gifts bestowed from my father, and reach people in a different way.

Though it took years for me to admit it—to myself, and most especially to my family—I had finally mustered the courage to tell the truth, and go after my dream. In America.

I knew that I was meant to make a difference in people's lives, though I didn't know exactly how. I thought maybe I was destined to have a television show and be the next Oprah. For five years, I had been hustling, relentlessly, pursuing this dream. I tracked down Hollywood moguls, big shots, and movers and shakers in L.A. I stalked one at a yoga class, another outside of a restaurant, Steven Spielberg at his kid's soccer game; I crashed movie premieres, waltzed into the offices of top Hollywood talent agencies and demanded meetings.

I thought I knew what my life should look like and was hell-bent on making it happen.

But for all my work, all my striving, I felt I still had nothing to show for it.

Sure, I had led some seminars. I had produced a pilot. I had even done my own radio show. But I kept hitting walls and questioned why things were so hard and there was so much struggle in my life.

As I stared out that train window, I thought about the book I could fill with all the rejection I'd faced year after year. They say America is the land of dreams, and yet I was filled with memories of people laughing in my face, looking at me as if I were crazy, kicking me out of their offices, saying, "Never going to happen, kid."

It was heartbreaking. And I had had enough. My American dream felt over.

So I put all my things in storage and began to travel. I was on a pilgrimage to discover myself, my purpose. If what I thought I was here for wasn't what I was here for, then what was I really meant to be doing with my life?

I disembarked in Kerala, sweaty, exhausted, and

thankful to be on solid ground. I hoped this Gangoli character lived close by, so I could find him and then locate a place to rest.

I shouldered my backpack and began to ask around. *I'm looking for this guy, people call him Gangoli. He's an enlightened teacher.*

All I got were blank stares.

This was strange. Usually a guru has a following, maybe an ashram, people in town usually know who they are and where they live. But I wasn't having much luck. Finally, I walked into a corner store and approached the cashier who nodded his head, and pointed up the mountain.

"How far is it?" I asked.

"About fifteen kilometers," he said.

I looked down at the heavy backpack that I'd set on the floor.

"Is there somewhere to rent a moped around here?" I asked.

He smiled and directed me down the road.

Ten minutes later, I was on my way up the mountain, on an old, rickety moped.

As my moped tried to propel itself up the steep mountain, a small cabin appeared off in the distance. I pulled off the gravel road and parked. Shouldered my backpack, walked up to the front door, and knocked.

It was a bit surreal. From Hollywood to the jungle, how the hell did I get here?

The door swung open and revealed a man, small in stature, with white hair and glasses. He looked more like a schoolteacher than an enlightened being. He had no long beard, no flowing robe. But he greeted me as if he'd been expecting me.

"Hello, welcome. Come in, come in."

He ushered me inside and I looked around at the minimal furnishings. No one else was in sight. It was just this man, in this small cabin, deep in the mountains. Where were his followers? What served as his temple?

Is this what enlightenment truly looks like?

He invited me to sit at his kitchen table, and offered me a cup of chai. I began to tell him my story. I explained that I had traveled to India from the United States because the dream that I thought was my destiny wasn't manifesting. I told him about all my endeavors, and all my failures. I told him that, in fact, I was kind of mad at God. It seemed cruel to put this vision in my heart if it wasn't what I was meant to be doing.

He nodded his head as he prepared the tea. Finally,

he sat down and gazed at me over his cup, his brown eyes filled with light.

"You are mad at God. This is good!" he said with a laugh. "When you reach this moment, you are on the right track. This moment of frustration, of hitting the wall, is growth. The sense of *I've done everything I can and I'm done! I can do no more!* This is the beginning of a breakthrough. **Sometimes when you think you are lost, you are closer than you think.** When you have done everything you can do and there is nowhere else to go, there is nothing left to do but to let go."

"But why did I feel called to America if it was going to be this hard? I could have just stayed in London and taken over my father's churches. I don't feel like I'm doing anything significant right now, other than struggling to pay my bills and surviving. I don't feel like I'm getting anywhere. I feel so much inside, and yet it feels like I'm wasting my potential."

Gangoli set down his cup and looked me in the eyes. "If you think you can screw up life's plans, rest assured, you are not that powerful," he said. "This whole idea of *I'm not where I'm supposed to be* or *things aren't going according to plan*, those ideas come from your attachment to how *you* think your life should be."

He paused, his eyes twinkling. "This is just ego, Kute." He waved his hand as if the ego were a pesky fly, something you could just swat away.

He continued, "Your ego is attached to this idea of what it thinks your life should look like, and it is trying to force its way. Your whole identity, who you think you should be, the famous TV star, is wrapped up in this out-come, a television show. But what if life has different plans for you?"

He paused and took a sip of tea.

"When you are stuck in your ego, you are limited to its plans. *I want to be the next Oprah, and have a TV show. It's got to look this way or that way.* That is just a belief you have formulated for yourself. But just because you believe it, doesn't make it true. You have reached the end of what you can do. And now something bigger is seeking to hap-pen. When you stay attached to your ego's plans, you block your ability to be truly open to the magic of life."

I stared down at my cup. Could he be right? Was this the source of my suffering? My damn ego? In that mo-ment, I hated my ego and I wanted to kill it.

Gangoli looked at me intently, like he somehow knew what I was thinking. "We all have an ego, Kute. There is no problem with ego. The Dalai Lama has an ego. The pope has an ego. Letting go of ego does not mean you have to kill it. In fact, it's not that real to begin with. It just means your relationship with it shifts and you don't have to hold on to it and its plans so tightly. You are so much more than your ego, and what life has planned is so much bigger than what your ego can conceive."

He got up to rinse his cup in the sink, letting me sit with his comments.

With his back turned to me he said: "The ego thinks it knows how your life *should* go. When things often don't go according to plan, it judges your life a failure, and then tries to force a result."

He turned back around and sat down at the table. "It's time for you to do life differently. To move from being driven by your ego and its motivations, to something deeper. More real. More authentic. The old way you have been living your life is no longer working. **You think you've reached the end, but right now you are at a new beginning.**"

I nodded my head, slowly taking in his wisdom.

"You've got to take your ego out of the driver's seat. Stop letting it run your entire life."

He paused and gazed out the window.

"People come to me and want to know what they

need to do to be truly happy. They ask me how they need to change, what kind of meditation they should do; they are eager for self-improvement. But if you want to change yourself, you better hurry up and do it now, because when you're 'enlightened,' you won't give a shit! Because you know that the *you* that you are trying to change really isn't the *real* you anyway."

And then he began to laugh.

I couldn't help but join him. Because deep in my soul, I could feel that he was speaking the truth.

The reason I kept hitting a wall?

The life I was living was too small for what I was seeking to become. And the shoe no longer fit.

REROUTING

What if it wasn't supposed to be so hard?

What if we weren't meant to struggle and suffer and force our way through life?

When you are striving to prove yourself.

When you worry that you aren't enough.

When you are constantly comparing yourself to others.

When you're struggling, barely able to keep your head above water.

I invite you to consider that perhaps it is time to explore how the ego might be getting in your way.

Now, let's be clear. The ego isn't the enemy. To resist the ego is, in and of itself, ego . . . and keeps you stuck in ego even more. To exist in this world, you need an ego, a personality, a name, a role. It's okay. An ego is a necessary mechanism of our human existence and daily functioning. So don't judge it, beat it up, or fight it.

Instead, observe it for what it is.

It isn't the sum total of who you are. It is just a collection of all your beliefs, your labels, and your stories about who you *think* you are and how you think your life should be.

When we are children, we learn that certain behaviors help us avoid pain and receive love. Maybe you got a good grade one day and then were lavished with praise. You recognized that being "the smart one" was an effective strategy for feeling loved. It went in your collection of identities to cling to and set your compass for where you thought you were supposed to go in life. Maybe you were a child prone to making mistakes, getting messy, being too loud. Surrounded by messages that you weren't good enough, you began to believe you were inadequate. And that impacted everything that came after.

Though you start as a blank slate, with endless potential, by the time you are an adult you have been molded into a version of yourself that you think will help you get what you need: Safety. Love. Validation.

Who do I need to be in order to be loved? we ask.

And then we create "ourselves" based on our answer.

This coping mechanism is the ego. It helps us survive as children, but often ends up limiting us as adults.

What we are is so much more.

Growing up as the preacher's son, I became the good boy, the responsible one, the perfect son. I followed the rules, got good grades, and did what was expected of me, believing that this is who I really was.

But eventually, I felt the real me trapped inside. Imprisoned by the limited character I had become, I could only access a small portion of my potential. Not that I wanted to be bad. But being stuck in the role of the good boy meant I couldn't be anything else. Couldn't be angry, couldn't question the authorities—most important, couldn't follow my heart because it might disappoint people or rock the boat.

It boxed me in. For years.

Until one day, I woke up.

Realized that I was more than the good boy, the

preacher's son. And until I shed that persona, I'd never have the freedom to do what I felt I was meant to do.

I have news for you.

The ego is just a set of patterns that has been solidified over time.

It seems real, but it isn't.

And your personality is not permanent.

Those stories and labels are not who you really are. But if you buy into them, they will end up limiting you and become your reality.

So consider: If who you are is a story that you made up, whether consciously or unconsciously, then realize, you can *unmake* it, too.

FACT OR FICTION?

I had a client I was working with who truly believed that she was unworthy and unlovable. It was her constant mantra to herself and she went out of her way to prove just how unlovable she was. She would push away people who truly loved her, self-sabotaging relationships so that she could keep her belief about herself. *See*, she would say? *He left. People don't love me.*

When we began to work together, we discovered that

this belief came from an event that happened in her early childhood. When she was just five years old, her mother left. Just picked up, moved out, leaving her daughter with her father.

From that moment on, she believed she was unlovable. *If my mother loved me, or if I was enough, she wouldn't have left*, she believed.

When she told me this story, I looked at her with compassion.

"I want you to take a moment and consider that story that you have been telling yourself for years. Is it true? Have you spoken to your mother? Did she confirm that she left because you were unlovable?"

"No. I never saw her again after that day."

"So what if your interpretation of that event is inaccurate?"

"What do you mean?" she said, confused.

"An event happened and you interpreted it to mean something about yourself. *I'm unlovable*." I paused. "What if she didn't leave because you were unlovable? Maybe she was addicted to drugs and she didn't want to put you through the pain of watching her struggle. Maybe it was actually her love for you that caused her to leave."

She looked at me quietly.

"Or what if she left because she knew that she was not ready to be a mother, that she had emotional issues to deal with before she could love you the way you deserved to be loved? What if she left because she had an issue with your father? And it had nothing to do with you? What would that mean for who you perceive yourself to be?"

She looked down at the ground, tears brimming in her eyes. Then she shook her head. "No, every man I've ever loved has left me, so it isn't just my mother. This is who I am."

I looked her directly in the eyes. "*I'm unlovable* is not who you are. It's the identity you have created for yourself, what your ego believes yourself to be. Those men left because either they weren't available or ready for love, or they had their own issues to deal with, or possibly you wouldn't *let* them love you the way they wanted to love you. You pushed them away with your belief that you are unlovable."

She frowned, still resisting what I was saying.

"You see, when things happen to you, you give those events meaning to make sense of the world. You create beliefs about yourself based on your interpretation of those events. Then you hold tightly to those beliefs, and they become your identity. But that isn't who you truly are. That is your ego. Your ego is a collection of beliefs and stories and interpretations that become your identity, who you believe yourself to be. The more attached you are to your identity, the more in your ego you are, the less room you have to experience yourself or life differently."

She looked at me as tears streamed down her face. "No, but my mother told me *you're unlovable!*"

"Even if she said that, her words don't make that reality. That may be her belief based on her own hurt, because hurt people hurt people. But just because she said it doesn't mean it is true. It is just something she said."

"But I saw her . . ." she began.

I stopped her in her tracks. "Show me 'unlovable.' Where is unlovable? You are describing events that happened, experiences that occurred. Yes, that person left; yes, that person hit you, but you can't see 'unlovable.' A chair is in front of you. This table is in front of you. But 'unlovable' is not in front of you. It is a story in your mind that you made up. You can't show me 'unlovable.' It is just an idea. A concept."

I paused.

"It is time to let go of the story that you are unlovable. First, you have to see that it is just a story. Once you let go of that label, that story, that false self-perception, you can open up to a new reality. Of how lovable you truly are. That you are love itself."

She collapsed on the ground in tears.

It is not easy to let go of our long-held identities. Our ego wants to protect itself. It thinks it is protecting us! But it is holding us back.

What if who you are is not who you think you are?

Surrender the story.

Surrender the belief.

Surrender being right.

Surrender the attachment to the identity.

It's time to question your beliefs. We must recognize that our beliefs about ourselves are not the reality.

This is not easy to do. But to start the journey of surrender, we must first become aware of the stories we are telling ourselves about who we are, who we should be, what our life should look like, and what should be happening.

It is limiting you and how you experience the world.

MAKE SPACE

Imagine for a moment that you've just gotten into a devastating car accident. As you wake up, you find yourself in a hospital bed. You don't remember what happened. In fact, you don't even know who you are.

I walk into the room and tell you that your memory is gone forever. So I'm here to fill in the blanks. Your name is Sam. You've got a wife and three kids who are waiting just outside the door. You work at a financial planning company in Minneapolis. You love karate and Japanese food.

What would you do? What could you say? Who are you, if everything you know about yourself has been erased?

Really. Where did the *you*, that you were before, go?

Where is this you? What is this you? Where do you exist?

In that hospital room, with no memories, no stories, no beliefs, no history about yourself, what is the one thing you could know for sure?

Take a moment to consider. What could you know, for sure, beyond a shadow of a doubt?

You've been told who you are, what your name is, what your religion is.

But the only thing you could know for sure, at that moment, from direct experience is: I AM.

Not, *I'm not enough, I'm unworthy, I'm unlovable, I'm*

*a failure, I'm Johnny, I'm Kute, I'm Jewish, I'm Buddhist. I'm
a bad mother. I'm smart. I'm stupid. I'm not a creative person.*

Those are just labels, not the truth about you. You
would look around the hospital room. You wouldn't even
know what town you were in! But you would look around
and know: **I AM. I EXIST.**

All the things we put behind I AM are just concepts.
Just ideas. Stories. Some may be helpful. Some, not so
much. Some might be true. Some might be false. But
they are not who you truly are.

Don't get attached to the labels about yourself. Be
willing to surrender the labels that have limited you. You
are not your labels.

Think about the Dalai Lama for a moment. He
doesn't walk around all day, saying, "Check me out! Do
you know who I am? Look at me and how spiritual I am!"
He is not focused on what others think. He is not attached to the idea of what being the Dalai Lama means.
It doesn't determine his sense of self-worth or value. He
is not threatened by criticism or encouraged by praise.
He knows he is not his ego, so is at peace.

There is space between his ego and who he knows
himself to be. And therein lies his freedom.

We are often seeking this freedom through things

like alcohol, drugs, or sex. When you have a few drinks, the tight grip of your ego loosens and for a moment you feel free. No longer boxed in by inhibitions and self-consciousness. Maybe you get high, and all those things that were so consuming are no longer so important.

But it doesn't last.

Even through orgasm we seek a release of the ego. For a fleeting moment, the ego is gone. How blissful it is! In that moment of orgasm, the ego dissolves. The French call it "the little death." That is why it is ecstasy.

But once again, it is short-lived.

What we chase through those temporary experiences is available to us all the time.

There is freedom when you let go of ego. And realize that who you truly are is *soul*.

THE SHIFT

Ego will stay in a relationship with someone you know is wrong for you, forcing it to "work" because you think you *should* be together.

Soul lives in total honesty and integrity.

Ego attempts to do the more advanced pose in yoga class so you can look good.

Soul tunes in to what the body needs, knowing there is nothing to prove.

Ego desperately seeks what society deems success, even though it isn't what you are meant to do and still leaves you feeling empty.

Soul knows that true success is being who you truly are, and living authentically.

Ego plays small, hiding your light in order to please those around you.

Soul realizes that it's your true nature to shine. **And that you being you is the greatest gift you can give the world.**

When we let ego drive the show, we find ourselves on a never-ending treadmill of effort.

When you make the shift, you access infinite potential.

More power. More peace. More purpose.

It changes everything.

Then you are playing a different game.

Consider the caterpillar, crawling on the ground, enjoying life on its little legs.

Life is good. It's enough.

But we know that within the caterpillar is the potential to become more.

We look at the caterpillar, and say, *Don't you know what's available to you? If you just give up your caterpillar ways, you'll be one of the world's most magnificent creatures. Even more, you'll be able to fly.*

Nah, I'm good, the caterpillar says.

This is what the ego does.

It clings to our limited ways. It suffers. It stresses. It is always anxious. It's controlling.

There comes a moment when the caterpillar has to give up its earthly ways and go into the darkness of the chrysalis. The only way it can become who it is meant to be is to go beyond its current form. To go into the chrysalis, let go of its small self, so that it can emerge with wings.

If we insist on holding on to our life as we know it, we too will remain a caterpillar.

To surrender does not mean you hide away in the chrysalis for the rest of your life.

No. To surrender is to release the old. To surrender is to enter the chrysalis. To know that on the other side, there is something greater.

This is when we can move from a limited life to one that is truly unlimited. And begin to open to the infinite possibilities that life has to offer.

METAMORPHOSIS

I spent a month with Gangoli, in the lush paradise that is Kerala. I would wake up each morning and drive my rickety moped through the winding streets to his cabin. We would sit and drink chai, or take a walk along the riverbanks. I would come back in the afternoon. More talking, more questions, more listening. He showed me that even without any trappings of success, you could live a life filled with meaning. That happiness isn't about having millions in the bank, being a famous TV star, or possessing a Lamborghini. It's about being at peace with yourself, knowing who you really are. And living each moment authentically and fully.

One day, as we watched the sun set over the mountains, he looked at me and said:

"Everything unfolds exactly as it should. As it is meant to happen, even if you cannot see it at the time."

He paused. "Kute, I'm so thankful for this time we have spent together. I hope that it has allowed you to recognize that what you've been going through the last five years only looks like failure from the perspective of your ego. But when you realize that you are much more, that you are a soul, here to have a human experience, then your real purpose is to grow and evolve. Then, everyone is your teacher and in every experience there is a lesson that you can learn."

We turned to walk back toward his cabin as he continued.

"Everything in life is conspiring for your soul's growth and evolution, Kute. Sometimes not getting what you thought you wanted is truly a gift that you may only understand later. So whenever you are going through a challenging moment, ask yourself: How is this serving my highest growth? What am I meant to learn from this? **How is this situation a blessing for me?**"

He turned to look at me.

"Trust that what is truly meant for you cannot be taken away. And what is not meant for you cannot remain. If you try to hold on, you just block your blessings."

He shook his head. "You came here in search of an enlightened being. But no one is enlightened, because in enlightenment there is no sense of 'I.'"

I turned to look at him. I didn't really understand what he meant. He gazed up at the sky.

"Once you are enlightened," he continued, "there is no longer this sense of *my* life, there is only Life."

I too gazed out at the sky, knowing this man had taught me so much, and I would never be the same. I felt like he was pointing me to the magic.

I gave him a big hug as tears welled in my eyes with gratitude for his kindness, his friendship, and his wisdom.

As I got on my moped and headed down the mountain, the wind caressing my face, I realized how much I had obsessed over whether I was making the wrong move or the right move. In my career. In my personal life. Constantly stressing out, spending hours trying to make a decision, consumed by the thought: *What if I let people down? I've got to do life perfectly!*

As I thought of Gangoli and his wisdom, I wondered: What if I let go of the belief that I could ever make a mistake?

What if all mistakes are simply the ego's misinterpretation of reality? A simple misperception, because the ego can only perceive from one viewpoint.

While the soul sees the bigger picture.

What if there were no mistakes, and every single thing that had ever happened to me was a perfect piece of the puzzle of my journey? An essential ingredient to assist in the fulfillment of my life's purpose and why I was here?

I would no longer ask: *Am I making the right decision?* Regardless of the outcome, if I do it, I'm going to learn something, I'm going to grow, it is going to lead me closer to who I really am and where I am meant to be.

As I coasted down the mountain I realized that Gangoli was introducing a different approach to life. And it felt like freedom.

SET FREE

If you find yourself beginning to resist things that are happening in your life, stressing about a decision, or worrying about an outcome:

Stop.

Pause.

Breathe.

In the grand scheme of life, you can't make a mistake.

Yes, you can drop a glass and it shatters, and you shake your head. *How could I be so stupid?*

But if that experience teaches you to be more present, slow down, and take care of your surroundings, was it a mistake? Or a simple lesson?

Yes, you can hurt someone, unintentionally causing

them pain, emotionally or physically. But if you apologize, make amends, and vow to go forward more aware of your impact on others, was it a mistake? Or did it serve a purpose, too?

I'm not saying things are always easy.

I'm not saying people don't need to be held accountable for certain actions.

I'm not saying you won't have to face the consequences of your actions. This is life. There are karmic repercussions, there are legal ramifications. You can't ask God to get you out of the situation that you created in the first place. Surrender is to take responsibility and ownership to face what you created. Without judgment. Embrace the lesson and grow from it without being a victim.

Surrender is in fact responsibility. It isn't about escaping but being fully present with life.

Sometimes you've got to speak up, speak out, take someone to court, or ask for forgiveness.

Sometimes to surrender is to see where things have gone wrong and have the courage to demand justice.

But when we see things from the soul perspective, there is a kind of perfection, even in the imperfection. Even in the struggle. Even in the midst of the chaos of the human experience. We may not always understand from the perspective of the ego, in the moment.

I ask you: If you looked back on things in your life that in that moment seemed like a disaster—a job loss, a relationship ending, an injury—can you imagine, now, not having gone through those things? Can you look back and see the intricate design of your life, and how it led you, perfectly, to this day, to this moment, to these words on the page?

This is what it means to give up the idea that you can make a mistake.

That day, the wind at my back, I felt like I'd let out a deep exhale, like I'd finally stopped holding my breath, like I was finally able to actually enjoy life . . . rather than suffering under the ego pressure of *got to do it right, can't do it wrong.* Without that realization, I never would have felt the freedom to try new things in my life. Begin to take clients to India. Make videos to reach people online. I could be so much more creative, and fluid, and innovative once I gave up the ego pressure of perfection.

So surrender the idea that you can make a mistake.

You can't make a mistake.

You.

Can't.

Make.

A.

Mistake.

Enlightenment is really freedom, the freedom to be who you truly are. It's not some woo-woo experience on a mountaintop. It is realizing you cannot miss your destiny if you tried. And living each moment as it comes, with awareness and acceptance.

CLAIM YOUR WINGS

Consider Nelson Mandela, a living embodiment of the magic of surrender.

Nelson Mandela was one of the greatest men to have ever lived. He came to symbolize the freedom of a people. The resurgence of a nation. He became a symbol of liberty itself.

How did he lead such an epic life, become a legend, an inspiration to so many?

He made the shift I'm inviting you to make: from ego force to soul power.

Mandela did not set a goal when he was a child to become this great political leader. "I cannot pinpoint a moment when I became politicized, when I knew I would spend my life in the liberation struggle," he writes in his autobiography. "I had no epiphany, no singular revelation, no moment of truth, but a steady accumulation of a thousand slights, a thousand indignities, a thousand unremembered moments, produced in me an anger, a rebelliousness, a desire to fight the system that imprisoned my people. There was no particular day on which I said, From henceforth I will devote myself to the liberation of my people; instead, I simply found myself doing so, and could not do otherwise."[1]

This is surrender.

Surrender isn't passively accepting the status quo. Surrender is daring to not only feel the injustice but to do something about it.

Real surrender is not a matter of form. What you wear, what you don't wear, what you do or don't do, what you say or don't say.

Surrender is an inner state of being and your relationship to life. A commitment to follow where life leads you. Sometimes it leads you beside quiet waters. Other times it leads you straight into the fire.

But surrender is the knowing that wherever life leads you, there is a reason, you are ready, and life will back you up.

People pilgrimage to the jail cell in which Mandela spent so many years. They want to see where a man did not give in to despair, but became more convinced of his purpose.

More of a leader.

More of a visionary.

More available.

Even as he remained behind bars.

Perhaps we seek to have the impact of Mandela, but we forget that he spent twenty-seven years in prison. But he was not suffering the entire time he was locked up. Resisting his arrest, resisting his imprisonment. He trusted that it was part of a plan. A plan that was bigger than him.

Was the imprisonment right? Was it just?

No. But did it ultimately, in time, lead to the liberation of a people?

Mandela did not have a master blueprint for the kind of legacy he left. He had no whiteboard timetable on the wall. *Okay, I'll get arrested here, and then be in jail for a few years.* Should he have been released after two years, I'm sure he would have loved that. But life had other plans. And he trusted life would unfold the way it needed to.

Mandela didn't know if he would die in jail. But he was willing to.

He surrendered his idea of what he thought his life should look like. To make room for life. To become available.

This gave him access to greatness.

Surrender didn't mean that he accepted apartheid. He was not passive. He felt called to fight the injustice that surrounded him. But he surrendered to how the fight would unfold. He wasn't focused on it happening on his time line, securing freedom only for himself. He was focused on freedom for his people.

When we force life, instead of letting it unfold, our imposition on life is our limitation on life.

Mandela's sister also knew that her brother belonged to life. "I realized that he isn't ours, he doesn't belong to the Mandelas. He belongs to the nation. We have given up my brother because we see from his nature he was meant to embrace the whole nation. . . . We can see this is the job God gave him."[2]

Real freedom is surrendering to the life you were truly born to live.

Surrender is not about giving in or giving up. It is

understanding that true power comes from partnering with life. When we surrender to who we are really meant to be, we become stronger, not weaker. Dare I say it, we become superhuman. And we elevate our impact.

So.

Stop resisting your calling.

Stop refusing your greatness.

Stop dimming your light.

Stop hiding your gifts.

Stop fighting your purpose.

Stop arguing for your smallness.

Stop crawling in the mud.

It's time to say yes to the real reason you were born.

This is when you access the magic.

And then life will give you the wings to fly.

CHAPTER TWO

LEVEL UP

LIES

WE GLORIFY SAINTS, but they live in remote lands.

We worship the angels, but their feet do not touch the ground.

We celebrate superheroes, but they're not real.

But to be truly human, in this world, is what takes true courage.

It takes courage to be who you truly are in a world that is always trying to get you to be someone you are not.

It takes courage to speak up in a world that just wants us all to get along.

It takes courage to be in this life fully, with all its messes, its ups and downs, light and dark, sweetness and bitterness.

Perhaps this is why so many of us turn away from the call of truth. It's easier to stay skeptical, be jaded, live in the mind, hide behind sarcasm, erect walls of defensiveness. It's easier to play small and protect ourselves from the disappointment of living full out, with all its risks.

But if you want magic, truth is the key that will set you free.

Happiness is simple. But it isn't always easy.

To be happy you must acknowledge the truth.

Tell the truth.

Speak the truth.

Live the truth.

If all you did today was to fully tell the truth . . .

Your life would transform.

STRIPPED DOWN

I was nineteen years old.

And had somehow landed the woman of my dreams.

She was much older than me. Stunningly beautiful. Spiritual. Smart. When I first saw her, I was much too intimidated to talk to her, feeling she was out of my league. But we ran in the same circles, and eventually, through a series of fateful events, we were introduced. We developed a friendship and it was clear there was a deeper connection.

And we fell in love.

At the time, I thought it was the real thing and convinced myself that there would never be another woman like her.

But just six months into the relationship, I began to have this sense. You know that sinking feeling you sometimes get when something isn't quite right? Like maybe someone isn't telling the complete truth, or maybe it isn't a good idea to make that investment, or maybe you shouldn't go on that trip?

Well, despite how perfect she seemed and how much I loved her, I began to sense very early on that maybe this relationship wasn't going to work out.

How did I sense this? Well, this beautiful woman, who had so much to offer, whom I loved beyond measure, would often become extremely jealous when I'd talk to other women, talk about other women, or even glance in their direction. It got to the point where I felt like if I even breathed around another woman, she was furious. It triggered her and she would punish me with the silent treatment, withholding her love. After experiencing this a few times, in order to avoid her feelings of insecurity, I began to suppress my naturally outgoing nature. I would timidly remain by her side, close myself off to other people, so that she didn't have an opportunity to get jealous and react.

Honestly, I didn't even realize I was doing it. But this was how I thought I could keep her happy and retain her love. It makes me very sad to think about it now.

I shut down a part of myself so that I could make the relationship work.

Of course, deep down, if I thought about it, I was miserable. But I couldn't fathom letting go of the woman of my dreams. I was addicted to the identity of us as a couple. The story I made up in my mind and was so attached to was that she was the only one for me.

So despite my intuition telling me that this was not going to work six months in, we dated for four and a half years.

That's right. I spent four and a half years being in a relationship that I knew probably wasn't going to work, and instead tried to fit myself into a box. These were years that I was struggling to build my career and make my dreams happen. And yet how could I, when I was holding so much of myself back?

There comes a point when the truth catches up with you. When you can no longer run from it, and it confronts you head on. **The truth is, you can't run from your truth. It will catch you every time.**

You might think: Well, I'm not ready to deal with it. But you don't realize you are dealing with it, right now, in your life.

For me, my truth stared me in the face when, at two p.m. on a Tuesday, I found myself in a strip club in North Hollywood.

I was twenty-three years old. I had never been to a strip club before. I was a preacher's kid! But whenever my girlfriend got jealous, she would withhold sex. This went on for weeks or months at a time, for four and a half years. I tried to convince myself that spirituality was more important than sexual connection, but I realized that I was just denying my human nature. Denying my need for physical connection. With each denial, I was lying to myself even more. About who I was, and what I needed. Pretending to be something I thought I needed to be.

I completely shut off from my own truth.

So there I was. Staring up at the stage in the strip club in shame. Feeling like *What the hell am I doing here?*

But in our darkness, we can sometimes see the light. It was in that moment, in that dark club, music blasting, bodies gyrating, neon lights flashing, that I realized I could no longer deny my truth. I knew that I had to break up with her and I could no longer live in this prison of my own making.

I walked out of that strip club, sobbing, but finally in touch with not just the truth, but the action I now knew I needed to take.

I mustered the courage to tell my girlfriend how I felt, and we broke up immediately, in dramatic fashion. It was one of the hardest things I've ever had to do. I really thought my life was over.

But instead, my life began.

As soon as I left her apartment with the truth having finally been acknowledged, after the initial shock, and grieving, I felt free.

And I realized that nothing and no one was worth my freedom. If I don't have myself, then I don't have anything. And the love that you get by being someone that you're not never feels truly fulfilling, anyway. Because the version of you that they are loving isn't the real you.

I vowed from that day forward never to suppress the truth of who I am again.

TAKE TRUTH TO TEA

Maybe you too have remained in a relationship that you knew was wrong. Tried to convince yourself that you should be grateful, that things might get better, that you can keep trying to make it work.

Or maybe you've stayed in a job that was not right for you, under a boss who was demeaning and was not going to let you rise to your potential.

Or maybe you kept pursuing a college degree just to please your parents.

It's okay to find yourself in a situation that isn't right for you. It happens to all of us, even the best of us. But the difference between those who dare to be great, and those who settle for lives of soul-numbing status quo, is what you do with the truth. Do you squash it and stay where you are?

Or do you dare to acknowledge, listen, and follow its call?

If you want to experience the magic of surrender, you must be willing to stop pretending. To access your power, to discover your purpose, to start to live a life that feels right, you must make friends with your truth.

Sometimes people think to succeed in life, you've got to BS your way to the top. But take it from one of the most successful men in the world: "Truth—or, more precisely, an accurate understanding of reality—is the essential foundation for any good outcome."[1]

These words come from multibillionaire Ray Dalio. Dalio is the founder of the investment company Bridgewater Associates, one of *Time* magazine's one hundred most influential people, and one of *Forbes* magazine's one hundred wealthiest people in the world. Called "the Steve Jobs of Investing," he built his company from the ground up based on a number of principles that guide his own life.

One of them is called *radical transparency*. It is a commitment to truth. It is a call to not filter one's thoughts but to share them, openly.

Here is why he believes in it so fiercely: "Imagine how many fewer misunderstandings we would have and how much more efficient the world would be—and how much closer we all would be to knowing what's true—if instead of hiding what we think, people shared it openly," he writes. "I'm not talking about everyone's very personal inner secrets; I'm talking about people's opinions of each other and of how the world works. I've learned first-hand how powerful this kind of radical truth and transparency is in improving my decision-making and my relationships. . . . I practice it as a discipline and I recommend you do the same."[2]

Unfortunately our world doesn't teach us transparency. It teaches us to cover up, hide who we are, deny what we feel, and pretend to be someone we're not.

But it isn't really working, is it?

I want you to consider the freedom that is available once you acknowledge the truth. Surrender the lies. See each situation for what it truly is.

What would happen if you invited truth to tea, sat down with it, offered it some pastries, and then faced it head on?

What is the current state of your relationship, for real, no excuses? And how does it make you feel?

What is the state of your physical health?

What is the reality of your financial situation?

What do you *really* want to do with your life?

Who were you truly meant to be?

Trevor Noah, the host of *The Daily Show with Trevor Noah*, discussed our human tendency to hide on Howard Stern's radio show. As they talked about dating, Trevor said: "How many people go into a relationship like a used car salesman, bullshitting about what they want? *I love long walks on the beach! I love adventure!* You don't love adventure, you hate white water rafting, you hate leaving the house! Be honest. Say, *I like sitting on the couch watching too much TV and I'm a slob,* and then if somebody goes, *I love that,* you have now found true love."[3]

We do not need to be used car salesmen in life, spinning a tale, trying to get people to buy into what we are selling. We do not need to pretend.

It's time to surrender the lies.

I know it may seem scary at first. But once you let go of pretending and start to live authentically, you will never want to live any other way.

HIDE-AND-SEEK

When I created the Liberation Experience back in 2006, I wanted to create one of the most transformational and life-changing experiences on the planet, to help people get in touch with who they really are. It was a trip to India where a client would be with me, one-on-one, 24/7, for twelve days straight. They wouldn't know what was going to happen. They didn't get to call any of the shots.

They had to let go of control, to surrender, from the very beginning, if they were going to get anything from the experience at all. They had to write their will, letters to all their loved ones, just in case they didn't come back. That's how fully surrendered they had to be to the experience.

When Jonas embarked on the plane, he had been complaining of feeling down, depressed, and stuck. He didn't know what the issue was and hoped that we might unpack the cause during the twelve-day process.

The first task I give my clients once they board the plane is to write their entire life story during the long flight. I want them to think about everything they've been through, all the ways they have defined themselves, and hear how they tell the story of their life. For many, the process of unraveling who they are begins there as they face their past, sometimes for the first time in decades.

When we landed, Jonas handed me his notebook, the pages filled with his sprawling handwriting. As we caught a cab to the town where we would begin our adventure, Jonas began to talk about his life. And he kept bringing up his father. How important he was in his life, how influential he was in the person Jonas became, and, ultimately, how much Jonas wanted to make him proud.

As he talked about his father, his eyes lit up and his movements became more animated. It was like he came back to life.

When we arrived, we wandered out into the marketplace. The sights and sounds of India surrounded us, and we stopped talking as we took it all in.

We paused in front of a stall selling brightly colored fabrics, and Jonas touched the intricate weavings. Despite our lively surroundings, darkness had descended upon Jonas once again.

"Jonas, you were just a joyous man on the car ride. But your light has been dimmed again. I know that you were once a happy man, proud of all you've accomplished with your business, and filled with love for your wife and children. So what happened?"

He looked down at the fabric in front of him, his fingers trailing the pattern.

"I don't know," he said softly.

I stood next to him and put my hand on his shoulder. "You are safe here on this journey. To feel it all. To fall apart. You don't have to hold it all together and be the strong one who takes care of everyone else. You don't have to do that here."

He turned away from me.

"What happened, Jonas? It is okay to admit the truth. Until you do, you will feel stuck. If something happened that you haven't dealt with, you'll just remain stuck in this place until you acknowledge it."

Though he was still turned away from me, I felt his shoulders begin to shake as emotion that he had been holding back caught up with him.

He turned toward me and his eyes were filled with tears. "My father," he began, before he began to cry uncontrollably.

"It's okay," I said quietly. "This is good. Let these feelings out. This is what has been waiting to be released."

He tried again and took a deep breath. "My father died six months ago. It was so sudden, a shock to us all. One day he was alive and the next he was gone. I didn't even have time to say goodbye."

He paused as he let more tears fall.

I guided him to a bench on the outskirts of the market, so that we could have some privacy and hear each other speak.

Jonas sat down and stared at his hands. "I had to be strong for the family, for my mother, for my sisters. I was the one handling all the details, making sure everything got done. When I got back to L.A., I just"—he paused—"I just kept going. Pretended nothing had happened. Until just a few moments ago, I had . . . I had never even cried."

He wiped his cheeks and sighed. I could tell he felt lighter, after finally admitting what was going on. He continued, a thoughtful expression on his face. "I think I worried that if I felt the sadness, that it would engulf me and I would be paralyzed, unable to work, unable to tend to my family. So I just kept going. But after about a month, I felt so down and depressed and like I was just a shell of a person."

"Jonas," I said, "you have to grieve for your father."

He gazed out at the market in front of him, so full of life, vibrant, busy. Life went on, no matter that he wanted to hit pause and forget everything that had happened.

"Kute, if I grieve him, if I feel those feelings, then I have to admit that he is really gone," he said, and he began to cry again.

"Jonas, your unwillingness to feel the sadness will not bring your father back. I know that you think denying sadness will allow you to deny the reality. But your father is dead. You loved him deeply. The love will never go away. In fact, if you allow yourself to grieve fully, you'll feel closer to him than you do right now, trying to pretend that he is just a phone call away."

I paused.

"All feelings remain present until fully felt, Jonas. The more you deny them, the longer they remain. Once acknowledged and given space? They dissolve. They have done their part."

He nodded quietly and let the tears fall.

"Give yourself permission to feel the pain fully. You think your heart will break. But it will break open to a bigger dimension of love than you knew before. Love is bigger than form. When your father died, the form of the relationship changed, but that doesn't mean the love is gone. Nor does it mean he is no longer with you. He may no longer be with you in physical form, but the real essence of who he is, is spirit. His spirit is beyond form, which means it is always connected to you. The real relationship that you have with him is an inner connection, and not even death can take that away. He doesn't have to be gone. He can still be here, in your heart."

Jonas closed his eyes and took a deep breath.

"Yes, Jonas, keep your eyes closed and place your hand over your heart. I want you to visualize your father. Take a moment, right now, to express everything you want to say to him, all that you never got to express, until you feel complete."

Tears were streaming down his face. He didn't yet have words. But then I saw him take a deep breath, and begin to speak to his father.

I gave him time and space. To fully sit with his feelings.

Once he was finished, we walked over to the nearby beach, and we gazed out at the shimmering ocean.

"Every time you begin to miss your father, remember that he lives in you. He will live on in you and through you in how you live your life. The best way you can honor him is to live the most authentic life possible. So even though you can't touch him and see him physically, the loving is accessible inside you. Close your eyes, go inside, and he is always there."

Jonas wiped a few more tears that had escaped. He took a deep breath. "Thank you, Kute. I was just so afraid to feel those feelings. But even now, I can tell that denying them was zapping all of my energy. I already feel so much more light and free."

Each day we were in India, Jonas accessed another layer of unexpressed emotion. Feelings that he had been denying. This had been a pattern for him—not just since his father died, but for many years before that. But as we accessed those buried feelings, of sadness, anger, grief, and fear, they were released. And he was able to return home, not only lighter, but no longer fearing his feelings. He had a new approach to life.

Pay attention and acknowledge what is going on inside you.

Make friends with those feelings.

They aren't as scary as you think. Unless you feel your feelings in a healthy way, they will end up expressing in unhealthy ways. You can't outrun your feelings. You won't be able to escape them. Nor should you want to.

Feelings are pointing to where more freedom is available, if you are willing to be honest.

EMOTIONAL EXCAVATION

How are you distracting yourself from the truth?

How are you letting yourself stay stuck instead of facing the truth and doing something about it?

Suffering is a signal from the universe.

It is time to surrender to our feelings.

Too often, we try to hide from our suffering or even deny it is there. But your suffering is your gold. Your unhappiness is your treasure. I want you to look for your suffering and consider its message.

What could it be trying to tell me?

Instead of convincing yourself that you aren't suffering, recognize that your suffering is showing you what is in the way.

It is highlighting areas for growth.

I'm happy enough at work. Maybe the truth is: *I hate my job. I was made for more. I'm going to stop pretending that this job is enough and admit that I want to do something different with my life.*

Until you acknowledge the truth, you can't take steps to change your current reality.

He'll change. Will he? Or is this a lie you're telling so you can stay in the relationship? *Okay, he probably won't change. Am I okay with things exactly as they are, rather than being in love with his potential? No. I don't like it. I deserve more.*

If you don't face the truth, you can't take the necessary action to break it off and be open to a relationship that actually fills you up.

I'm not smart enough to have that career. Is that really true? So often our beliefs are lies, but we've never taken the time to give them a reality check. *Where did I learn that? From my mom, belittling my ambition. But is that true? I don't know. Maybe I'm smart enough. I'm no longer going to buy into that lie. I'll let that go and be open to the idea that maybe I am capable of going after my dreams.*

These are the ways our lies hold us back from the next level of our lives.

So pay attention to your life. Don't numb yourself, distract yourself, stay so busy that you can't hear the truth whispering to you in moments of quiet. Life is constantly sending you signals. Stop pretending things will get better, taking a pill to suppress the feelings. When we ignore our feelings, good or bad, we miss out on what they are trying to tell us.

Let me be clear. I'm not talking about indulging or wallowing in negative feelings. This is to be a victim. Surrendering to our feelings is not succumbing to our feelings. Succumbing is when you collapse into them and let them take over, rather than being fully present with your feelings, and experiencing them with awareness. To surrender to your feelings is to recognize the feelings and sensations that are present within you, without judgment. To not be in denial of the feelings but acknowledge them and allow them to be, to inform, to send their message and then move on.

I know that to acknowledge your feelings, especially the negative ones, may go against every strategy you learned as a child. Maybe it wasn't safe to express feelings in your family. When you did, you were yelled at, or told *Boys don't cry*. So you learned to suppress negative feelings.

But feelings are just energy, neither good nor bad. Feelings are pointing to where more freedom is available if you are willing to be honest.

So, surrender to the feelings. Sometimes it is painful.

But the short-term pain is better than a lifetime of suffering.

MESSAGE RECEIVED

That relationship when I was nineteen was not the only time I found myself in a relationship with someone who was jealous. Throughout my twenties, no matter how different my girlfriends were in age, looks, background, and interests, they each had that one defining quality. I would complain to my friends: "What is the deal? Why do I always attract the jealous ones?"

But my complaining did little to solve the situation.

Complaining is an avoidance of truth. Complaining is an abdication of responsibility. Truth requires taking responsibility for how you feel and the actions you take. **It is only when you are responsible for yourself and your life that you can change your life.**

After the breakup of yet another relationship, I took a trip to Spain to walk the Camino de Santiago, a 500-mile trek through the mountains of southern France into northern Spain. People have been walking the Camino for hundreds of years. Everyone from Dante to Pope John Paul II to St. Francis of Assisi have been said to traverse its terrain. Some people believe the entire trail falls along a ley line, one of the earth's energy meridians, so there is a spiritual energy you have access to as you walk its path.

Most of the time I hiked alone. But one day, I walked with a man named Eduardo. He carried a heavy pack, and was one of the fittest people on the trail. As we walked, I began to talk about my relationship struggles, in particular these jealous girlfriends.

After listening for several minutes, Eduardo said: "Hey man. I want to ask you a question."

"Sure," I said, happy to answer anything. "Ask away!"

"I hear you complaining about how frustrating it is to be in a relationship with a woman who is jealous. Yet you keep attracting them. They keep flocking to you like bees to nectar. So, let me ask you. *Why do you want to be with jealous women?*"

What was he talking about? I *didn't* want to be with jealous women. That's what we had been talking about. "Man, I don't want jealous women!"

I was furious with what he was suggesting.

"Kute, that may be what you say. That is even what you *think* you believe to be true. But reality tells another story. And reality doesn't lie. We attract to us what some part of us wants, deep down. If you want to attract something different, you will have to be honest with yourself."

I slowed my pace as I tried to decide whether to continue this ridiculous conversation.

He turned around and looked at me with a knowing smile. "You keep attracting jealous women, which must mean some part of you wants to be with jealous women. Unless you own this, you will stay stuck. Don't judge yourself for it. Just get curious. There is a message for you in your suffering. Ask yourself: 'What am I getting out of being in a relationship with a woman who is jealous?'"

I looked down at my feet, stepping carefully over each rock. *What was I getting from it? A lot of frustration and angry fights and no sex! That's what!*

Eduardo walked wordlessly next to me as I considered what he could mean.

Could I really want to be with jealous women? If so, why?

I had spent so much time blaming the women for the strife I felt they were causing me.

But in this moment, if I was honest, I couldn't deny that I was the common denominator in each relationship.

Sure, I could argue with reality. But I wasn't going to win.

Okay, okay. Let me own the truth.

It was hard for me to admit to myself. *I want a jealous woman.*

This sounded crazy. It went against everything I believed about myself. It was uncomfortable to take ownership of my own reality. But only once I admitted the truth, could I do the work to investigate what was going on and truly heal. And as I got curious about the truth, instead of judgmental about it, I began to realize the answer.

"You know, Eduardo, I never really thought about it, but I think I've had my own fears of abandonment. I think I was terrified of being left alone. So if I was in a relationship with a woman who was jealous, then she was the one who was needy and possessive, and deep down, it made me feel wanted and liked. It gave me a false sense of security."

Eduardo's eyes lit up, and he patted my back like a proud teacher as we continued to walk. "Yes, Kute! Being with these women was a protection mechanism. You wanted to keep your heart safe."

I nodded as my pace quickened. I couldn't believe this. My ego had wanted to keep me focused on them. *There is something wrong with her!* And distracted from the truth.

But the truth was, being with jealous women made the little boy in me feel safe.

It was a hard pill to swallow.

But as they say, the truth will set you free.

Eduardo walked alongside me. "If you truly love yourself and accept yourself as you are, then you won't need validation from someone else. You won't fear being alone, you won't fear being rejected, because you will know that being yourself is the greatest gift you can give the world. You won't need to change yourself to get love. You will just be yourself and be love. Then you have nothing to lose."

I cannot tell you how freeing that conversation on that trail was for me. Sure, I had realized that I was suffering in my relationships, but I had never taken the time to explore exactly why that was. Accessing the message of my messy relationships allowed me to acknowledge the part of me that was afraid of being left; the part of me that thought I still needed to pretend to be someone who I was not in order to be loved.

It changed all of my relationships going forward.

And I learned to make truth my friend.

WARNING BELL

Imagine if the fire alarm was going off in your house and instead of going and checking the stove, you put your headphones on and turned on loud music. You distracted yourself from the loud noise, instead of investigating and taking action.

This would be insanity.

And yet we do it in our own lives. All the time.

Our feelings are our fire alarm. Our suffering is our signal.

When we deny the signal of our feelings, we just continue in situations that are not good for us. Before we know it, our window for taking action has closed, and the house has burned down.

Surrendering to your feelings doesn't mean you lie down and cry. It means you call the fire department. Get your kids out of the house. Grab your important documents and then get to safety.

Surrender is not denial. Surrender is facing reality.

Surrender isn't being powerless. It is being empowered.

It is only when you surrender that you can truly know what action to take next.

I get that it can feel overwhelming, even scary, to face your feelings and acknowledge your truth, some of which you may have been denying for many years now. But if you want to be free, you must be more committed to the truth than what you have. You must want the truth more than you want what you think you want.

Here are six questions that I have used for over a decade with thousands of clients to help them get in touch with their truth. They are like a laser tool to drill down to the essence of what you really feel.

I call it the Truth Process:

1) What lies am I telling myself?
2) What am I pretending not to know?

3) What is the payoff for staying stuck?

4) What has the lie been costing me?

5) What am I afraid might happen if I tell the truth?

6) What right action can I take today?

Here is how it works in action.

When Jim walked into my office, he sat down with a sigh. He had recently come to the realization that his wife had never been the right person for him. He had known it from the start, but had ignored that truth because to break up would have meant starting over, admitting failure, and he had been ready to settle down and start a family. Ten years into the marriage, nothing had gotten better, and he knew no amount of work would turn her into the right person for him.

It was time to move on.

But Jim had three children. He didn't want to break up the family.

Jim and his wife had decided that it would be better if they had an arrangement that they would stay together until the kids were grown and out of the house. So they were living in a loveless marriage that had run its course, pretending that everything was okay.

"Kute," he said with exasperation, "I don't understand. I've been doing so much work on myself, and really trying to create what I want for my life. Why am I still not happy?"

I smiled. "Jim, you can't be living an inauthentic life and be happy. The two don't go together. So if you are still miserable, something is off. We've got more to uncover, a truth to unearth. Let's go excavating. So, ask yourself: What lies am I telling myself?"

He looked at me, confused. "I'm not telling lies. I've told you that I no longer want to be with my wife. I've told her that. So I'm no longer living a lie."

"You have admitted that you no longer want to be married to your wife. That's a wonderful first step. But there is another lie. You think that you can just put your life on hold while you wait for your children to grow up. Can you really do that and be happy?"

He looked at me, exasperated. "This is what we need to do for our family. For the children's sake."

He was resolute in his insistence.

"I understand why you want to hold on to the familiar family structure. But staying in something that isn't right for you won't make it right. And it certainly won't make you happy. All the little strategies that you use to distract yourself from the fire alarm going off in your heart—gambling, occasional affairs, TV, alcohol—they won't bring you the true happiness you are seeking. They may distract you from the pain for a moment, they may drown out the noise, but the only thing that will bring you happiness is to acknowledge the truth about what you need to do."

He crossed his arms in frustration and wouldn't meet my eyes. "I just don't want to deal with it."

"But, Jim, you are having to deal with it, no matter what. The unhappiness in your life is you dealing with it. Whether you deal with it or don't deal with it, you're going to deal with it! There is no escaping. Until you acknowledge the truth, you'll just find yourself in this cycle of denial and resistance and unhappiness."

He stared out the window.

"Okay. Fine, I am not in love with my wife anymore. And I will never be truly happy while I am still married to her."

"Good," I said with a smile. "Now you know what you need to do."

"No. What do you mean?" He looked up at me, eyes filled with fear.

I took a deep breath. "You are just pretending that

you don't know what to do. That's a comfortable place to be, because it requires no action. But you know what you need to do."

He began to protest. Usually when faced with the truth, the ego will resist. Because there is something to let go of, and the ego wants to hold on. Resistance to the truth is the ego's protection mechanism.

I looked at him with compassion. "The truth will set you free. And you hold the lock and you hold the key."

I paused. "You think that staying for the kids is helping them. But remaining in a loveless relationship is setting an example for your kids that this is love. Is this the kind of relationship you want for them?"

He shook his head.

"Maybe before you are ready to take action, you have to admit what is comfortable about staying. The payoff you get."

He looked at me, anger rising. "There's no payoff. There's nothing I'm getting out of it!"

"If there was no payoff, you would have left already. Just consider what you receive from staying. Comfort. Companionship. Security. Those things are good. It is understandable that you want that. Make friends with the part of you that refuses to let go. Embrace it. Love it.

Appreciate it. Acknowledge it. Listen to its concerns. It has been your friend, trying to get you what you think you need. But perhaps you don't need to protect yourself in the same way anymore."

He gazed out the window, attempting to hold back tears.

He nodded quietly. "You're right. Those things are comforting and hard to let go of."

"So now, ask yourself: What has the lie been costing me? How has it held me back and kept me from all I desire?"

This one was easier to answer. "Well, it has kept me from feeling free, from feeling happy. I feel like I've hit pause on my life until the kids are grown. And then I resent them. I feel bad that I feel like they are the reason I'm not happy right now."

"They are not the reason you aren't happy. You are. Because you refuse to let go and level up. What are you afraid will happen if you tell the truth?"

"My kids will be screwed up. They'll be mad. They'll never forgive us."

"Maybe. But consider. What if the greatest gift you could give your children was to be truly happy and fulfilled? To show up for them fully, because you are being who you truly are? What's important is that they know that you love them unconditionally. That regardless of changes, they will have two parents who will be there for them, no matter what. Couldn't you accomplish that while still telling the truth?"

"Maybe," he said quietly.

"Acknowledge the fear that has been holding you back. That fear *may* come true, but it may not. Once you can get comfortable with the worst-case scenario, and make peace with it, it frees you up and no longer holds you back."

He considered this, picturing what the worst case scenario was.

I lowered my voice and gently continued. "You can't live their lives for them. All you can do is live your life the best way you know how. And pray that living truthfully, living fully, living authentically, will help them do the same."

He looked at me, relief washing over his face.

"Okay," he said with determination.

"Okay," I said with a smile. "Finally, the last question is maybe the most important. What action can you take today to begin living the truth?"

The tears began to fall. The relief of admitting the

truth was freeing, a rush of emotion long held back brought to the surface and released.

He walked out of my office knowing his next step.

Jim called me later that day. He'd talked to his wife. Surprisingly, she was relieved that he wanted to stop pretending. Despite their fears, they sat down with their kids and told them the news, with love and compassion, emphasizing that nothing would ever alter their unconditional love and support.

Jim admitted that he was nervous about how it would all play out. But he also felt the seeds of happiness beginning to take root. He felt free. He felt empowered. He felt alive, for the first time in years.

Fast-forward to six months later. They had respectfully ended their marriage. Jim had fallen in love with the love of his life, the kind of love he'd always dreamed of. His ex is the happiest she's ever been.

And their kids? They weren't just fine. They were better than fine. No longer living where the toxicity of untruth was permeating every single corner of the house, the kids were finally able to witness their parents happy and being honest, with themselves and each other. There was no need to act out anymore because everyone was dealing with the issues head on.

Truth ultimately serves everyone, even though it may not always seem that way at first.

The truth makes everyone face reality and deal with the situation as it is.

And when you deal, then you can heal.

THE CALL OF TRUTH

Maybe, like Jonas, you are denying the pain because you are afraid of the consequences of acknowledging the truth. Or maybe you find yourself in a pattern of financial struggle. Can you get curious about why you find yourself in this place and what the payoff is? What do you get from struggling financially? It seems counterintuitive, but sometimes there is a payoff. I had a client whose father kept bailing him out when he would run out of money, and it was his unconscious way of feeling close to his father. It provided a connection to his father and he worried that without it, he wouldn't feel loved. Until he admitted the truth, he was going to stay in the cycle of struggling financially.

Maybe you have a dream that you keep deferring. You keep finding reasons to put it off. There is a fear that you haven't examined. Think about the worst-case scenario of what might happen if you went after what you truly wanted. Make friends with that situation, and then take action, knowing that you will be okay even with the worst-case scenario.

I had a client who acknowledged that her worst-case scenario was running out of money and having to go back to the same job she was doing now. It was like a light bulb went off when she realized that she was already living her worst-case scenario, in this moment!

Surrender is not sitting on your meditation cushion.

This is inactivity.

Surrender is not making excuses for your inaction and procrastination.

This is laziness.

Surrender is not ignoring your daily needs.

This is irresponsibility.

Surrender is total responsibility and commitment. To show up. Face life fully.

So you can make choices that can bring about change.

This is what it means to live an authentic life.

You stop pretending. You make it a practice of inviting truth, in all aspects of your life. With yourself. With your friends. With your family.

And then you take action, no longer being stuck in the same place you've been for years. You take responsibility. And then level up.

It impacts our personal lives. And even more, our world.

Bryan Stevenson is the founder of the Equal Justice Initiative (EJI) and author of the best-selling book *Just Mercy*. He founded EJI in 1989 to challenge wrongful convictions and unfair sentencing in his home state of Alabama. Alabama has the highest death-sentencing rate of all fifty states and does not have a public defender system. He saw firsthand how many people were not given a fair shot. Were not given a voice. One in nine executed inmates end up being innocent. He didn't want more innocent people to die.

Since then, he has been fighting for the truth to come to light.

He fights for those wrongly convicted. He strives to overturn unfair sentencing, and reveal how racial bias impacts prosecution.

He is committed to the truth. He wants us, as a society, to stop denying our painful history, but to recognize how it still impacts our present. To acknowledge how our unwillingness to examine our past impedes our progress today. It keeps us stuck in a pattern of prejudice and injustice.

He calls for a reckoning. A wake-up. A change.

This is surrender to the truth.

Bryan is just a regular guy who made everyday decisions to follow the truth, to prioritize truth. This is what makes him great.

He does not descend from the gods. He doesn't possess a special gift. What makes him great is every choice he made, despite the risk, despite the consequences, despite the unknown.

And it changed the course of history.

We can make these choices too.

Many people look the other way. Some people expect others to step in.

But to surrender is to realize that you are the one the world has been waiting for. A commitment to the truth will change everything about your life. It will set you back on course and allow you to finally access who you are meant to be.

It may not be easy. But to follow the truth is always worth it.

When Bryan had the chance to meet the legendary Rosa Parks and Johnnie Carr, architects of the

Montgomery bus boycott, and described what he was attempting to do through his organization, Ms. Parks leaned over and said: "Ooh, honey, that's going to make you tired, tired, tired."

Then Ms. Carr reached out her hand and said: "That's why you've got to be brave, brave, brave."[4]

To surrender does not mean there will not be fear. But that fear does not hold you back from doing what you know to be right.

Twenty years after he founded EJI, Bryan Stevenson's book has been on the best-seller lists for over two hundred weeks and has been adapted into a feature film.

Bryan has given his life to this work. His work is not quickly accomplished or even always celebrated.

And yet, he will continue.

When he talks about how he does it, he says: "You learn to trust what your heart tells you about what you have to do. You learn to stand when everyone else is sitting. You learn to speak when other people are quiet because you have to do the thing that advances justice, advances what you believe in."[5]

What would happen if we were all this committed to the truth?

If we were all as brave at facing the truth, and using

it as our guiding compass? In our own lives. And in our world.

#BlackLivesMatter.

#MeToo.

#NeverAgain.

Let me be clear. Surrender is not about dropping out or going up to live in the mountains in seclusion.

Surrender is about daring to show up. And living in this life fully.

Surrender is about no more wavering. No more one foot in and one foot out.

But total commitment.

What would happen if we all fully surrendered to the truth, in our lives and in the world?

Quite frankly, it would change everything.

CHAPTER THREE

THE ULTIMATE IMPROVISATION

CONTROL

LIFE IS FULL of unexpected surprises.

And success is never a straight line.

You don't always need to know where you are going to get to exactly where you need to be.

How many times have you thought something was going to happen, and then it didn't, and it ended up being the greatest gift? How often have you looked back over your life in astonishment at how an event unfolded perfectly even though you had no idea what was in store? Meeting your spouse, getting that job, running into someone you didn't expect, which led to a perfect opportunity. Did you plan those seemingly random moments?

You couldn't have planned some of the best moments of your life if you tried.

There is this idea that you must know your plan, your direction, and your outcome before you even begin. That you must have all the answers or have it all figured out.

This is a myth.

To surrender is to be open to what you don't know.

To surrender is to stop trying to force your way.

Surrender is the art of allowing. So that there's space for the universe to show up.

Surrender is acknowledging that you weren't really in control to begin with. Surrender is the art of letting go.

And letting go leads to more.

PIT STOP

I learned this lesson in the Indian train stations.

The trains in India are never on time. They arrive whenever they arrive, and it is rarely at the scheduled time. Until I realized this, I would show up at the platform thirty minutes before the designated departure time, my eyes on the horizon, expecting to see the train approaching at any moment. Maybe it was my Japanese sense of punctuality. I had places to go! Things to see! A schedule to keep!

But there was no train.

Why wasn't the train here? When would it come? What's wrong with this country? Why can't things just show up on time?

Oh, how I suffered on those platforms. Sweating, pacing, stewing in my thoughts about why this shouldn't be happening.

One night, my train was scheduled to leave at nine p.m. I was planning to get some sleep on the train, and was very tired after a long day. I looked at my watch. I had already been waiting an hour. I heard announcements over the loudspeaker, but I didn't understand the language.

I looked around me. The platform was a swarm of people. Surrounding me were sounds and smells and sights in all directions, like a colorful carnival. But I noticed that no one else was anxiously pacing, like I was. Instead, they seemed to be at peace. I turned to my left and saw a family of seven sitting on the ground. They had laid down a blanket and arranged a spread of Indian food. They were eating, chatting, and laughing. They seemed so happy, as though they were in heaven.

And here I was in hell.

When I traveled to India, I wanted to understand what it meant to surrender. And it was as though India was smiling at me, saying: *Are you sure you want to learn surrender? Okay, here you go. Let's start with a nine-hour train delay.*

No, that's not exactly what I meant. I wanted some blissful, movie moment, on a mountaintop with a monk!

We don't always get to choose what the lesson is, or how the lesson shows up. But we can determine how we go about learning it, and whether we actually get the message.

Around midnight, I had been waiting three hours and couldn't believe it. I hated India and its inability to be predictable. I finally walked up to a man who was reading a newspaper and drinking some chai.

"Excuse me, but do you know when the train will come?"

He looked at me, amused. Deep down he probably thought I was crazy. Was he some sort of oracle who could see into the future? No one had a crystal ball to know when the train would show.

Instead he folded up his newspaper neatly and said, "The train comes when it comes."

I looked at him in frustration as if to say: *Thanks a lot*.

But he continued, "Sometimes on time is not always on time. Your timing is not always divine timing. When things are delayed, don't always think that you're late. Everything has its own timing."

He then turned back to his newspaper, as if to say: Lesson complete. But I knew, in front of me, through this man, life was speaking to me.

We struck up a conversation. His name was Amir. He was middle-aged and lived in Mumbai. We are still friends to this day. Because Amir opened my eyes to how my resistance to life was creating my reality. Heaven or hell? Happiness or frustration? The choice was mine.

As we talked, Amir gestured to those around me. The family had long ago packed up their picnic. They had shifted around their luggage, snuggled up against it, and gone to sleep.

"You see, Kute, they are at peace. They have accepted that the train is not here. By resisting this fact, you only suffer. But when you accept it, then you can respond appropriately."

He shifted on the bench, making himself more comfortable. "They trust the train will show up eventually. Until then, they are enjoying the moment. They will eat, sleep, laugh, and be together. Why don't you do the same? Stressing is a waste of this moment. And it won't make the train show up any sooner."

He put down his chai and invited me to sit down next to him. "You can't control when the train is going to show up. What you can control is what you do on the platform, and how you live the moments as you wait. How you meet each moment of your life and how you relate with those around you. I invite you to embrace what's happening as it's happening. Heaven or hell is not outside of you, on the platform. It's in your mind. It's not about where you are out there, but where you are in here," he said as he gently tapped my forehead.

He smiled, and said: "Freedom is an inside job. Welcome to the Indian train station."

I was in awe at the simple wisdom he shared with me. The more I embraced it, the more the train station transformed. It morphed from a place of suffering into a temple of wisdom. The more I let go and allowed things to be, the beauty of the moment, which had been there all along, revealed itself to me.

We sat and talked all night and time flew by. And when the train finally did arrive, nine hours later, it was as though I didn't want to leave.

We think that everything needs to happen on our timetable.

And suffer when things don't.

True freedom comes when you realize that surrendering control of what is not in your control transforms your relationship with life itself.

GET RADICAL

Take a moment to consider how much of the suffering that you experience stems from your desire to control how things are going. From your demand that situations be different than they are.

Traffic. Your boyfriend's inability to commit. Your body. Your boss being a certain way. Your paycheck. The political climate. The inevitable delays in life.

Does your resistance to how things are actually resolve the situation? Is it really effective? Does it change the outcome?

Of course not.

Once you are done resisting, the situation is exactly the same.

The only thing resistance accomplishes is to ruin the moment.

As I thought about that family enjoying their picnic, savoring their feast, just sitting with one another, no schedule, no to-do list, telling stories, I was overwhelmed with sadness. Because I couldn't remember the last time I had experienced that with my family.

In fact, the kind of connecting that family enjoyed on the platform, I didn't share with my mother until I learned she was dying.

It is one the greatest regrets I have. That I didn't spend enough time with my mother, just enjoying the small things. I missed so many "picnics" with my mother because I thought I needed to catch the train. I left my mom "on the platform" in my desire to get to some other destination.

Resistance robs us of the ability to embrace all that life is trying to offer if we would only open our eyes. And look around.

So what would it take to give up your resistance?

There is another way.

Let me let Lady Gaga tell you about it. The famous Grammy-winning artist, and an Oscar-nominated actress, has sold millions of records and sold out arenas across the globe. But her journey has not been easy. What many people don't know is that she has struggled with chronic pain for many years, to the point where it was almost debilitating.

She shared her story of how she learned to deal with her pain as she sat on the stage with Oprah. And she shared the unusual advice of one of her doctors:

> [He said]: *You need to radically accept that you are going to be in pain every day.*
>
>   And I was like: *Are you f&*%ing kidding me? That's how I'm going to heal? By just accepting that I'm going to feel awful all the time? That I'm going to be in head-to-toe pain constantly?*
>
>   And he said: *You have to radically accept it.*
> And guess what? It took a little while, but I did, and you know what happened after that? Slowly the pain dissipated . . . and then all of a sudden, I could function.[1]

Lady Gaga says that accepting her pain changed her life. Rather than waking up every day fighting her reality, resisting it, trying to control it, change it, overcome it, she has learned to accept her pain, which allows her to access the power it was trying to give her all along: to become more than a superstar, but a messenger of hope for the millions who struggle with chronic pain alongside her. When she accepted her pain and learned to surrender to it fully, her pain transformed from a burden to a blessing. It finally revealed its purpose.

This does not mean she does not feel pain, or that there aren't sometimes hard days. But she is no longer suffering, in resistance to her reality. She is no longer trying to negotiate her way into a different situation.

So let me suggest that to experience the magic of surrender, we must stop our resistance, and surrender the illusion of control.

CONTROL FREAKS

At its heart, resistance stems from us wanting things to go our way. We want the train to show up on time. The promotion to come when we want. The pain to disappear immediately. To have a child exactly the way and on the time lines we always planned.

We begin to negotiate with life and try to make it do what we want.

Growing up in the church, I saw that sometimes even our prayers become negotiations and trades with God. A way to control our lives through our spiritual practice.

We get fixated on life being a certain way in order for us to be happy.

This just makes you a slave.

Events don't have to go a certain way for you to be happy. That is an illusion.

That belief stems from attachment to ego and what it wants. But remember, who you truly are is a soul, and there is a bigger picture than you can currently perceive.

What if you don't need to be in the driver's seat to get to where you need to go? And in fact, in a few years, with self-driving cars, you really won't!

I once dated a girl who was a total control freak. Everything had to be a certain way, otherwise she would stress out. She would get so emotional and upset at what seemed like the smallest things not going her way.

As we spent more time together, I understood that she was addicted to control because when she was a child, her mother was incredibly abusive. At a very young age, never knowing when the shoe would drop and her mother would lose it, she learned that if she could just control herself, control the household, control her surroundings, maybe her mother wouldn't get as angry. She did all she could to keep everything neat, tidy, and in its place so that her mother wouldn't explode in rage.

This was why she was seeking control in every aspect of her life.

That understanding gave me so much compassion for her desire for control. But I also knew that she no longer needed to keep everything in its proper place. It was okay to loosen the grip on control. Otherwise, she would always be a slave to life.

Control is one of the survival mechanisms we develop as children, in an attempt to avoid pain. When we first came into this world, we had all our needs met in our mother's womb. We could trust our environment. And then, boom! We were born and our needs stopped being met. Our parents were human, so maybe they were distracted, or disconnected. They didn't always give us what we needed. Gradually, we began to lose trust. Our survival instinct kicked in. *I never want to feel that pain again! Let me do what I can, to manage my life, so that I feel protected.*

Control mode: engaged!

Now, our desire for control has a positive intention—to keep us safe. But the way it goes about trying to keep us safe is limited. **In our desire for control, we often end up controlled.**

Be understanding of your little child self. You didn't

have the resources or skills to change your situation at that time. You may have felt helpless.

Consider that your current-day control strategy is just a reaction to that helplessness.

Control has a place, but it isn't the answer we think it is. We have worshiped at the altar of control, making it the god of our life.

There is another way. You can honor and love and appreciate that part of you that learned to control, and still take it off the altar. It has done a good job. It meant well.

But it doesn't have to be the driving force of your life any longer.

There is so much more available when you let go and begin trusting life. Even just a little bit more. And allowing yourself to be more open to what life has in store for you.

Surrender isn't just for the nuns and the monks. Lady Gaga is a powerful, successful, talented artist having a global impact, in the real world. Yet even she acknowledges that surrender has been an essential ingredient to her success.

Remember when I said letting go leads to more? On that couch with Oprah, Lady Gaga said: "When I talk to God . . . I say, tell me what to do. . . . tell me what to say, tell me how to say it and help me see the path and if you show me the path I will walk down it. . . . Look where that path led me. I am sitting right next to you."[2]

Can you see what is possible when we surrender? For those of you who might be afraid and thinking the worst, that you won't get what you want, or you are going to end up broke, single, and homeless, think again. I may not have a crystal ball to tell you where surrender is going to lead you. But for Lady Gaga, it led her to Oscars, Grammys, the next level of her purpose, and a seat next to Oprah. It will lead you somewhere magical. And the journey along the way will be one hell of a ride.

Surrender doesn't always have a neat and tidy resolution. Sometimes surrender means you take action and other times surrender means you wait. If you are in a job you hate, surrendering might look like fully accepting that you hate your job. Even if you don't quit, because you have a wife and kids and a mortgage, it is powerful to acknowledge and accept what is. Then you can surrender to the fact that you need to stay in your job for the moment, out of duty and responsibility to your family. Rather than complaining and resisting, you radically accept, you tell the truth, you focus on what you are grateful for, you do your job with excellence, learning the lessons that you need to learn where you are, fully knowing that this is not your final destination.

This is what surrender looks like in real life. Because you are no longer resisting, you will be open to following the signs when it *is* time to leave.

I know surrender can seem scary. That loosening the grip on control can feel terrifying.

But just imagine where surrender might lead you.

If you can surrender control, you can open up to new paths, new possibilities, and an even greater purpose unfolding.

LOOSEN THE GRIP

I had a client whose daughter had been struggling with alcohol addiction for years. Sam wanted, more than anything, to see his daughter get sober. To help her, he would pay her bills, clean up her mistakes; he even funded the launch of her business.

But this only enabled her addiction. And she didn't even appreciate it.

Deep down, Sam worried that he was not a good father to her growing up. To alleviate his guilt, to make up for what he didn't do, for the father he never was, he tried to rescue his daughter from her current pain. He didn't realize that his actions meant that she could always remain a little girl and a victim because she knew Daddy would come and save her.

Sam tried everything. But no matter what he tried, she didn't change. She wasn't taking responsibility for her own life and he wasn't allowing her to. So the cycle kept repeating.

It can be hard as a parent to let go of a child, and surrender that they have their own path to take and that you cannot learn the lessons for them.

But they have to do it for themselves. And allowing them to learn it the hard way takes true love.

One day, Sam sat down with me and I could see the weight of responsibility was still sitting on his shoulders. He needed to let her go. Letting go would not mean that he didn't love her. But true love is to allow someone their journey. True love means honoring another person's process. True love means no longer trying to control, but to release another person and let them live their life without our manipulations and ideas for what their life should be.

He was gazing out the window, a faraway look in his eyes.

"I know it is hard to see your daughter in so much pain and destroying her life. But you've tried everything and it hasn't worked. Even though you might be right about what you think she needs, it's her journey."

"But I don't know how to let her live her life, if she keeps making mistakes."

"I know they feel like mistakes, but this is part of her journey. Your job is to let go of your idea of what you think her life should be. There will be grief. And that's okay. That doesn't mean you stop loving her. What I want you to focus on now is not just her life as it is today, in the struggle and the pain. I want you to see her soul. Her soul is perfect. So even though she is doing some of these things that seem so destructive, if you are able to see her soul and see her perfection, then when she looks at you, she will see you, seeing her. Not the addiction, not the addicted person, but who she really is. And that will be a reminder to her on a very deep level. The greatest gift you can give her is to truly love her, and to truly love her is to truly see her."

"But, Kute, she needs to get sober! I can't watch her live her life this way anymore."

"Sam, you want her to be sober. But she is not sober

right now. Stop resisting that and radically accept that right now, she is an addict. You stepping in to try to take responsibility of her life just enables her. You rob her of the lessons she needs to learn, Sam. You think you are helping her, but there is a difference between helping her and truly loving her. Helping her only disempowers her in the long term."

He nodded, tears in his eyes.

"Sam, I want to share with you a prayer of surrender that I was inspired to write when I was in India, feeling stuck and ready to give up on my life and my dreams. I had just gone through a heartbreak; nothing seemed to be working out. And I wrote this. I want you to put your hand over your heart, close your eyes, and think of your daughter as you say these words. And I know you will feel lighter. I want you to visualize your daughter, see her soul, say goodbye, and let's say this prayer."

I surrender my need for control.
I surrender the way I think life should be.
I surrender my desire that things be different.
I surrender.
Thank you, universe.

I surrender my need to know.

I surrender my need to be known.

I surrender my need for other people's approval.

I surrender my imperfections and need for things to be perfect.

I surrender my goals and my desires.

I surrender ego.

I surrender I.

Thank you, universe.

I ask for everything that is not in alignment with my highest path to be cleared away.

I ask only for the highest good to be made manifest in my life.

I surrender everything.

Thank you, universe.

I surrender.

Once Sam stopped stepping in, without her father there to rescue her, eventually his daughter hit rock bottom. And it was only at rock bottom that she was finally able to admit her need to get help. She got into rehab, and was able to begin the process of healing and recovery.

Surrender is not easy. But the best things in life do not come easily. Surrender is a process: Of radical acceptance. Of letting go of the illusion of control. Of opening up to the fact that maybe, just maybe, you can release your grip—and your desire to force your way.

When we force, we are just reinforcing our lack of trust in the universe. We are back to our childlike ways, of trying to control the outcome to protect ourselves.

But I want you to consider the freedom that is available when you surrender your need for control.

I want you to consider that even though the unknown is scary, it is also beautiful. That you can make friends with the unknown. **Because you realize that you don't have to know where you are going, to get to exactly where you need to be.**

If you knew the outcome of every moment of your life, like a script, would it be any fun? I mean, if you sat down to watch your favorite basketball team, and you knew exactly what was going to happen every single minute, would it even be interesting? No! You'd turn it off! Part of the fun is that you don't know what is going to happen.

This is what it is to be alive.

TRUST FALL

A friend asked me the other day: "How does one trust when so much seems out of my control?"

I looked at him and said, "If you actually look around, how can you not trust? Every day, life is proving to you how much you can trust it!"

I know you may be like my friend. Uncertain that you can let go of control, scared everything will fall apart unless you hold it all together.

You want proof that you can trust? Bring your attention to the processes happening inside your body, right now. Connect with your breath. Feel how amazing your breath is. Notice how, like the ocean, it goes in and it goes out. Acknowledge the intelligence inside you that does that breathing. You don't force your breath in and out, twenty-four hours a day.

It happens. Without any effort on your part.

Each day, you take 23,000 breaths.

Your heart beats 100,000 times per day. During your lifetime it will beat 2 billion times.

Your blood travels 12,000 miles per day on its journey through your body.

Twenty-five million cells are being produced in your body every second.

You blink at least 15,000 times a day.

All of that is happening simultaneously in your body, at this very moment.

Without your effort.

What is it that does that? What intelligence keeps you alive?

Could that intelligence that keeps you breathing, every second of every day, perhaps know exactly how to unfold your life?

Consider nature, the sun rising and setting. Has there ever been a morning when you woke up, and it was still pitch-black outside? The sun just forgot to rise?

No. The sun rises, day in and day out. Without your input.

Is this not proof that you can trust the universe?

So if this innate intelligence has been unfolding life for billions of years, if it has been keeping you alive for as long as you have been on this planet, couldn't you trust life, instead of fighting it tooth and nail?

You versus Life. Who do you think is going to win?

It doesn't have to be a battle.

Surrender does not mean that you give up what you

want. But that you stop trying to dictate how it all happens.

FORCE VERSUS FLOW

This is what Bruce Lee was talking about when he said to be water.

"Empty your mind, be formless," he said, "shapeless, like water. Now you put water into a cup, it becomes the cup. You put water into a bottle, it becomes the bottle. You put water into a teapot, it becomes the teapot. Now water can flow, or it can crash. Be water, my friend."[3]

To be water means flexibility. You adapt. Water is still water no matter what vessel it is poured into. It does not worry when its form changes. When you hit water, it doesn't break.

It moves out of the way.

People think surrender is weak.

Was Bruce Lee weak? Absolutely not. But he knew that our power comes not from hardness and inflexibility but from our ability to mold and move and adapt accordingly.

Not every fight is the same. Not every punch requires the same response.

So when you find yourself struggling or trying to force your way, I want you to instead be water. Flow. Release control and ride the current. Get curious. What could life have planned instead?

Rather than focusing on what is wrong, how things aren't going your way, examine: What else is the universe cooking up? Observe yourself as a character in the movie of your life. Am I open to something better? Can I trust that if my plan doesn't work, something more is seeking to happen?

When you lose a job, rather than thinking your life is over, get curious about what comes next. You don't remain rigid, you step back and allow. What better thing could be coming in the next act?

A relationship ends, sure you may be sad, you may grieve, but you trust that nothing can take away what's truly yours, and if the relationship ends, something better is coming your way. John Steinbeck wrote to his son, who had just embarked upon a new relationship: "Don't worry about losing. If it is right, it happens—the main thing is not to hurry. Nothing good gets away."[4]

This is surrender. You don't try to hold on just because of history, and live in a museum of your shoulds. You don't try to keep something that isn't working just because it is what you know. Out of nostalgia.

You ask yourself: Does this light up my soul? Is this in alignment with who I am? Many times things drop out of our life and we get distraught, but it wasn't working in the first place.

What if you could trust that something even better was coming your way?

I watched an episode of *Comedians in Cars Getting Coffee* the other day, and Jerry Seinfeld was having coffee with Dave Chappelle. For a long time, Dave Chappelle was known as the guy who walked away from a $50 million Comedy Central deal in the midst of the third season of his hugely popular *Chappelle's Show*. People thought he'd had a mental breakdown. They speculated that he was on drugs. In reality, he walked away to save himself. He didn't like the person he was becoming. He went to Africa to get clarity, where he wasn't famous, he was just Dave. In that space, he realized that though he didn't know what would come next, he just knew what he was doing at the time wasn't right.

In one of his first public appearances after this period, he was interviewed on *Inside the Actors Studio*. And he said this:

"I don't know how this whole Dave Chappelle thing is going to end, but I feel like I'm going to be some kind of parable, either what you're supposed to do or what you're not supposed to do. I'm going to be something, either be the legend or a tragic f*%$ing story, but I'm going full throttle, going all the way! I'm eager to find out how this is going to resolve itself."[5]

Today, people are talking about his Netflix deal that paid him $20 million per comedy special. He has since filmed five.

In case you are wondering, that adds up to $100 million.

To some, it would be crazy to walk away from that $50 million deal, at the height of his success and popularity. But he knew it wasn't right for him anymore. And he had trust that something else would reveal itself. If it didn't, he was okay with that. But he knew nothing was worth compromising who he was.

As he and Jerry Seinfeld discussed his success, he talked about the difference between forcing and flowing.

"It's like the idea says, *Get in the car*," Dave says. "And I'm like, *Where am I going?* and the idea says, *Don't worry, I'm driving*. And then you just get there. . . . Sometimes I'm shotgun. Sometimes I'm in the f—ing trunk.

The idea takes you where it wants to go. . . . And then other times, there's me, and it's my ego, like, *I should do something!*"

"That's not good," says Jerry.

"No, because there's no idea in the car!" Dave says with a laugh. "It's just me. That formula doesn't work."

"If the idea is in the car honking, going *Let's go . . .*" Jerry says.

"Exactly," Dave says. "*I'm not ready!* you yell. *You can go like this*, the idea says. *Where are we going? What are we doing?* [you say]. *Don't worry about it. You'll see* [the idea responds]."[6]

Don't worry about it.

You'll see.

Those are words of surrender. Words of curiosity and openness. Availability. And thus, power.

I know it may sound like a different way of living. It's not what you've been taught. But so much of what we've been doing hasn't been working. This is why, out of my own pain of forcing and trying to make things happen, from years of career rejection and failed relationships, I realized that I needed to find a different way.

Now, it doesn't have to be all or nothing. I'm not saying you have to be like Buddha, leave the palace, sell all your possessions, and walk around in life with a begging bowl. No! You have bills to pay. Children to take care of. Real-world responsibilities.

But what if you got just a little bit more curious about life? What would happen if you were just a little bit more open, a little bit more aligned with the universe, a little bit more available, a little bit less attached to your way of doing things? What if you were willing to control just a little bit less and saw what happened?

I promise you, you would see some magic.

And then, you'd get addicted to surrender.

RIDE THE WAVE

Laird Hamilton began surfing when he was just three years old.

One of the world's greatest big-wave surfers, he dares to surf waves that most people would never even consider. I'm talking about waves that are seventy feet high. Waves that you must go out and seek in the middle of the ocean.

He is an innovator. He invented tow-in surfing, where a Jet Ski pulls you out to where the biggest breaks hit, sometimes miles out to sea. For a while he was scorned. People didn't think that was true surfing. And then they saw the kinds of waves he was riding. And trust me, they changed their tune.

From the very start, Laird was totally devoted to his craft. Surfing was his life. He has dedicated his life to the ocean. He never entered competitions, though it is fair to say he was arguably the world's best. He didn't surf for accolades and awards. He did it because he loved the art of surfing and wanted to see how far he could go.

He had a calling and he lived this calling every day of his life, because it was what he was born to do.

To me, that is surrender. And look where it took him.

His fearlessness and bravery have inspired millions of people. He has done what people would say is impossible, and has become a living legend.

It just goes to show how living a life surrendered to your unique path can lead you to heights of greatness.

When I interviewed Laird for my podcast, *SoulTalk with Kute Blackson*, he shared what it was like for him when he was surfing and it really struck me.

"You leave self behind. You leave 'you' behind. And you become part of something greater. The intensity of that perspective, of being part of something of that magnitude, it is all encompassing, all consuming. It swallows you in a way that you'd have to practice deep meditation for a long, long time to be able to maybe experience something like that."

He called surfing "the ultimate improvisation."[7]

This is surrender.

If you watch surfers, you'll notice that once they paddle out to the break, they don't immediately hop on a wave. They turn around and watch. Every wave is different. Some are big. Some are small. Some are good to surf. Some would crush them to pieces.

As the surfers wait for the right wave, they don't get angry or frustrated judging the waves. They sit on their boards, watching the sets come in, feeling the ocean, looking for the clues, preparing to ride the right one. But they allow the ocean to guide them.

Allow is the key.

Imagine if a surfer ran out into the ocean and tried to make the waves happen. Manifest the waves. Bring a hose and start spraying water around to make their own wave.

This would be crazy.

What if the surfer began to punch the waves, fight with them, got mad at them, yelled at them to be bigger, or smaller?

That would be insane. But this is what we do in life. Sounds crazy, right?

Once surfers understand *I'm not in control of the wave,* they can tune in to the wave and feel where it is going, allowing it to show *them* where it is going. Then they can partner with it and flow.

Yes, it looks like a surrendering of control. But the wisdom of those surfers is, they realize that they aren't in control of the ocean to begin with.

Let me be clear, surrender doesn't mean nonaction.

It doesn't mean being passive, doing nothing, or not taking responsibility for your part. It means you are following the clues, instead of trying to make something happen that isn't, or trying to fit life into your little box.

It means partnering with life, letting life lead you, and making space for life to show you where it wants to go.

Life is like the ocean.

To surf successfully, you must accept the ocean for what it is.

The great ones, the true masters, did not fight the nature of life. Life, like the ocean, is uncontrollable.

Surrender what is not in your control.

But surrender to what *is* in your control

Don't focus on changing the ocean.

Change yourself.

You have control over your response. Your words. Your actions. And how you show up.

Sometimes the waves will be small. Sometimes the waves will be erratic. Sometimes the waves will be hundred-foot monsters. Sometimes you get what you want. Sometimes you don't. Sometimes life goes your way. Sometimes it doesn't.

It's not the waves that matter.

It's how you choose to surf them.

No one can take this power away from you.

The ocean is never going to be flat. If your peace is dependent on the ocean being still, you will struggle every day of your life.

The ability to embrace all of life, not just parts of it, is where you'll find true freedom.

Deny it and die.

Surrender and ride the wave of your life.

CHAPTER FOUR

THE MIRACLE ZONE

POWER

WHAT IF I told you that miracles are not extraordinary?

That miracles are, in fact, simply the natural order of things?

When I say miracles, I'm not talking about turning water into wine.

I'm not referring to winning some impossible lottery ticket, or a far-out supernatural healing.

Sometimes we get so distracted, looking for exotic shamans and psychics speaking to the dead.

When we believe miracles are otherworldly, outside of our everyday experience, only for the select few or the holy ones, we deny the fact that they are actually right here in front of us, each and every day.

Let's stop looking for a miracle and realize that you are one.

Stop praying for a miracle and, instead, be one.

To be able to look into your child's eyes.

Is this not a miracle?

To be able to see the whole rainbow of colors.

Is this not a miracle?

To be able to make love and feel deeply connected with another person.

Is this not a miracle?

To see humans, who were literally strangers seconds before, coming together in the midst of a crisis.

Is this not a miracle?

Let's be clear. There is nothing ordinary about this life. In fact, when you simply focus on the miracle that is your very life, then you begin to realize the miracle that every moment already is, and has been all along. We just didn't see it. Then your eyes are opened to see and experience the profound beauty that is all around you.

I know some of you might be skeptical. I know some of you might want to rely on science and believe only that which you can verify, quantify, and measure with your mind.

But stay with me for a moment.

When we embrace the idea that miracles are not only possible, but that you are already living one, that you yourself are proof, then we become open and available to even more.

It's then that we begin to access magic.

THE MIRACLE MINDSET

Okay, let's get right to it. I've had more than my share of clients look me straight in the eye and say: "Kute, I don't believe in miracles. You can't prove them."

I get it. If I hadn't grown up the way I had, I'm not sure I would be open to them either.

But, look, I can't help it. Miracles are a part of my heritage. My father was known as the miracle man of Africa. For the first eighteen years of my life, I saw miracles flow from him, every single day. I don't know how they happened. I can't explain it to you scientifically. Yet I know what I saw with my own eyes. My father, touching a blind woman's eyes, restoring sight. Seeing my father say to a woman who had been confined to a wheelchair for years, "Stand up!"

"But I can't! I'm sick," she cried.

"Do you believe? If you believe, then stand up," he said, fearlessly.

I watched as she trembled, putting weight on her legs for the first time in years, and then standing up in awe.

But the miracles weren't simply limited to my father and his healings.

The fact that my mother and father, two people who were so incredibly different in every way, could stay married forty-plus years, despite their differences and the odds stacked against them, knowing that their souls had a purpose and a job to do. This was a miracle.

When I won a green card in an immigration lottery when I was eighteen, allowing me to come to the United States with no college degree, knowing no one. This was a miracle.

The time when I was so broke, not able to pay the rent, and about to be evicted, and that day, a check unexpectedly arriving from a client in the mail just in time. This was a miracle.

My life has taught me to be open to miracles. Because if I'm available and make space for them, they can meet me. And if I'm not, then I am the one who is blocking their flow.

You have to be open. Are you?

This isn't just some wishful thinking or some theoretical idea that I read about. This is the way that I have lived my life each day. Sure, maybe they haven't been tested in a lab, but I have rigorously tested these principles in my own life—with the risks I have taken, with the choices I have made, let me tell you. Life has repeatedly shown me. This stuff works.

Sometimes people say to me: "Kute, you're just so lucky. Everything seems to work out for you."

This is not the case. I have had some very dark times in my life, too. Many moments when I thought about giving up, wondering if I could continue.

But the key is, I've always been open and available in any given moment to something more than my mind can imagine.

Openness is the portal to miracles. That openness is your doorway to more. It is that availability to more that opens the flow of miracles in your life.

The miracle mindset is to be truly open to all possibilities.

We are the ones who are constantly putting limits on our life.

While life itself is unlimited.

We end up limiting what happens with our ideas of what we *think* can happen. Based on our past experience, our conditioning, the level of our consciousness, our attachment to our stories, we think we know what can happen, or not happen. To truly experience the miraculous, you have to be willing to not know. Which requires a courageous vulnerability. An innocence but not a naïveté.

The most amazing experiences in my life, I honestly haven't planned. There was the plan that I had, and then there was what actually happened. If I had held tightly to my plans, you probably wouldn't be reading this book right now. But I had to learn the hard way. After so many years of forcing my way through life, trying to make life conform to my idea of what I thought it should look like, I've learned to follow life's guidance. Even when I didn't understand. Even when I didn't know where life was leading me.

Miracles aren't something you have to make happen. Miracles are the natural by-product of what happens when you get yourself out of the way.

When you follow your inner guidance, you bring yourself into the flow and then life can unfold and deliver to you more than you could ever imagine.

OPEN YOUR EYES

I was doing a seminar one weekend when a woman stood up with a question.

"Kute, listen, you say there are miracles, but I don't understand how you can say that. Have you checked the news lately? Shootings, pandemics, wildfires. What about Jeffrey Epstein, and Harvey Weinstein? How can you still believe in miracles when there seems to be so much evil in the world?"

Humbled by her question, I realized what a complex problem she was identifying, one we all wrestle with. It was a big question, sometimes hard to get into in the midst of a weekend seminar. But I knew that the proper perspective on what our world is, and our place in it, can be key to surrender.

"Listen, I don't have the answers, but here are some thoughts. I'm not going to pretend there aren't difficult situations in this lifetime. I won't try to convince you that life isn't challenging, full of ups and downs. The reality is, this physical world is not some perfect utopia and it will never be. I'm not saying live in a bubble and be Pollyanna about life. But if we want to be free, we have to understand that life isn't perfect, and learn to accept the reality of this human existence. And as we begin surrendering to that, we begin to find a different relationship with life."

I paused.

"Don't look for perfection in this world. It doesn't exist here."

Here is what that means.

This world is a realm of interdependent, polar opposites.

Good and bad.

Light and dark.

Life and death.

Male and female.

Up and down.

Left and right.

Yin and yang.

It's the Tao. Life contains the whole. The entire universe is a manifestation of the Divine. And in the Divine, *everything* exists. Because the Divine *is* everything. So all possibilities exist in this world. Everything is contained within it. The sacred and the profane. The holy and the unholy.

Yet the divine, what we truly are, is beyond duality.

So to surrender is to understand and accept the nature of reality and to accept life *as it is*. Then you no longer resist it, fight it, and seek perfection in the imperfect. You no longer seek the infinite in the finite.

But let me be clear. To come to a place of acceptance of this world doesn't mean certain acts are acceptable, that we are condoning them or excusing them. It doesn't mean we don't try to make changes or better the world; that we don't try to end human trafficking or feed every child in need. But when we come to accept this world as it is, when we don't expect the world to be some perfect place, then, when it's not perfect, we aren't fighting it. We aren't in resistance. The expectation of perfection drops away and it frees us to stop resisting the world. When we can accept the world, then we can step into the world and make changes from the place of nonresistance.

This is key.

In fact, I believe that those difficult situations are actually calling us to step into our own power and goodness.

Stick with me for a moment. I know this is a big concept, but consider:

Without Judas, there would be no Jesus on the cross.

Without British colonization, there would be no Gandhi.

Without the sick and the poor, there would be no Mother Teresa.

So from the ultimate perspective, everything is perfect, even in its imperfection. At the highest level, Judas is in fact needed to play his karmic soul's role in the interconnected unfolding of the perfection in the cosmic play of Jesus's life. That doesn't mean there aren't real consequences for his actions. People like Jeffrey Epstein, Harvey Weinstein, the child abusers, the murderers, they will not escape their karma on their soul's journey. And neither should they escape the necessary justice that they have brought on themselves by their actions in this lifetime.

Rumi said: "Out beyond ideas of wrongdoing and rightdoing is a field. I will meet you there." When you understand that there will always be duality in this world, it doesn't make life easy. But it begins to open up the possibility to see life a different way, to see life from a bigger perspective. That may then enable you to let go of resisting the nature of reality so you can act from a place of centeredness and soul rather than ego reactivity. When you move from looking through the lens of the ego to that of the soul, it shifts your relationship with life.

Action may be necessary, but you can do so with less of the energy of against-ness. You are no longer giving power to the thing you are trying to change. It has less power over you. You are more centered in yourself, and then you are more likely to be more effective in creating the change that you seek. You can have more equanimity even during the hardest days.

This requires courage.

It takes true courage to not let your heart become jaded and hardened by the suffering in this world.

But consider that each and every one of us has the responsibility to control where we choose to place our attention.

What you focus on will expand. The media would love for us to stay tuned in to the negative cycle of the news and everything that is going wrong. Then we get jaded. We get skeptical. When we focus on all that is wrong with the world, we lose touch with what is beautiful.

And this is when we lose access to miracles.

This is what we must prevent happening if you want magic in your life.

It is a shift we all must make.

From bad news to good news. It doesn't mean you deny the bad. But you make a practice of tuning in to the good.

Did you know that every hour 125 million people have orgasms? That's two million each minute.

About 384,000 babies are born healthy each day.

Every day, 80,000 planes land safely.

Every year millions of trees grow thanks to squirrels forgetting where they buried their acorns.

You and I are literally made up of the dust of stars.

Life is still so very beautiful. Not because it is perfect. But because it *is*. Because you are here. When you focus on all that is broken, you start to disconnect yourself from the miracle that is your life.

What if you practiced, every day, acknowledging how amazing life is? Not because everything is going the way you wanted, not because everything seems perfect, but because life *is*.

This will give you access to the magic.

The colors of the rainbow.

The 8.7 million or so different species.

The unique combination of circumstances that allowed life to evolve on this planet.

Are these not miracles?

The gift of forgiveness.

The power in sobriety.

When people feel comfortable in their skin and celebrate who they are.

When you find love after having your heart broken so many times before.

These are everyday miracles.

We do not make or manifest miracles. Miracles already *are*. There is nothing to believe in. Our job is simply to remove our illusions and blocks that prevent us from recognizing them.

They are happening all the time.

Albert Einstein is known to have said: "There are two ways to live your life. One is as though nothing is a miracle. And the other is as though everything is a miracle."

We get to choose. Even this ability to choose is a miracle!

So are you ready to open to even more miracles in your life? There is a way of living that will bring you more into the flow. A way of life that allows you to be open, all the time, to where life wants to lead you. This is when you'll access the miracle zone.

And then you'll never want to live any other way.

GETTING OUT OF THE WAY

When I was in my twenties, I came home to London for a visit. I decided it was time to ask my father about his experience with miracles. I had never sat down to ask him how they happened, how he performed them, but now I wanted to know.

And he told me a story I had never heard before.

Many years ago, the former king of the Ashanti Region of Ghana suffered a devastating stroke and was paralyzed on one side of his body. He was flown to London to receive medical treatment. His family heard about my father, the miracle man from Africa, who had a church in London, and asked my father to come and pray for the king. My father visited him in the hospital and asked that they move the king to a house in London for a week so that my father could pray for him daily.

When my father walked into the room in which the king was resting, he sat down next to him and closed his eyes to pray. After a few moments, he turned to the king's wife, who was anxiously sitting by his side, intently offering up her own prayers. Out of the blue, my father was inspired to ask if they had any tomato juice. With a strange look on her face, the king's wife said she would

find out. A few moments later, she brought a glass of tomato juice in and handed it to my father. He prayed over
it and then asked the king to take a drink.

And as the king took a sip, the room was filled with
the sound of loud cracking. The king turned his head
toward my father, eyes wide as he swallowed the tomato
juice. *Crack, crack, crack, crack.* His body started realign-
ing itself. He jumped out of bed, waving his hands in the
air. "I can't believe it, I can't believe it!" he shouted, hug-
ging my father. This is the moment that they became the
best of friends.

I was as curious as you are. I looked at my father. I
wanted to know how this happened. Wouldn't you?

"Dad, how did you know the tomato juice would cure
him?" I asked.

"I didn't," my father replied.

"You didn't? So why did you give him the tomato
juice?" I continued, surprised.

"I saw an image of tomato juice in my mind's eye.
And I trusted that guidance. I had no idea what exactly
it would do, or if it would work. But over the years, I have
given up the need to know. I never question my guidance.
I've learned, Kute, that when I don't question my guidance, miracles happen. So my job is to get myself out of

the way. Let me be clear. I do not perform miracles. I do not heal anyone. People call me the miracle man, but it is God who does the miracles. Life does the miracles. They have nothing to do with me. What's my part? What's your part? If you want to know my secret, I just show up, listen, and say yes. It is much easier this way."

He looked at me, considering. "Kute, if I demanded to know how the healing would happen, what would happen next, how it would all work out, I would be anxious and stressed and maybe never take action. This is how we live life, the constant questioning. The constant questioning of the mind takes you out of the flow of miracles. If I don't do the miracles, why stress, why worry? It's not my responsibility."

I sat there stunned, recognizing the profoundness of what he had said. How our minds complicate things. I realized that I had been watching my father model this way of living my entire life. He did not question the guidance he was given. He didn't question when he felt called to marry my mother, whom he had never met. He didn't question when he was guided to start a church in London, with no money, miles away from his native Ghana.

He lived in a way where he didn't interfere with life. He trusted its guidance. Showed up and said yes.

What would it be like to live that way?

Here is what we do instead. We ignore the deep knowing in our heart. We distract ourselves from our deepest truth. We resist what our soul is nudging us to do. Maybe we feel guided to take action, but we want to know why. We want to know where. We want to know the answers before we take the first step. And so we sit, we wait, we hesitate. Then it's too late.

I want you to consider what might happen if you too stopped questioning. You too stopped interfering. I'm not saying you're going to be healing the sick, or making money grow on trees.

But when you get yourself out of the way, you get yourself into the flow. Then things in your life begin happening beyond what you can currently imagine.

You align yourself with the power of the universe.

LEARNING TO FOLLOW

I learned this firsthand when I walked the Camino de Santiago, the pilgrimage in Spain.

I heard many times before I left, that how you do the Camino is how you do life. That it exposes your patterns of control and resistance, and relationship with life.

When you begin, you check in at a small monastery in Saint-Jean-Pied-de-Port, France. There is no map. There is no GPS. There are no cell towers. No Internet. You just follow the trail. Dotted along the trail in random places are yellow arrows, pointing you in the right direction. Your job as a pilgrim is to find and follow the yellow arrows, trusting that they will guide you where you need to go.

If you don't, your mind will drive you crazy. Questioning. Doubting. Second-guessing. Destroying any sense of peace you might have on the trail.

There were times when I would spend hours walking, with no yellow arrows in sight. All I would be doing was judging myself, trying to figure out if I'd made a wrong turn. Other times I would see a fork in the road up ahead and before I could get there, my mind was obsessing over whether I should turn right or left. Projecting into the future, a hundred feet away, trying to figure out which way to turn.

There was no way I could know which way to turn until I got there. I needed to trust that the yellow arrow would be there when I arrived. What was the purpose of stressing here about what I would do there?

All I needed to do was put one foot in front of the

other, and trust that the yellow arrow would be there when I needed it to be there.

Isn't that like life itself?

Life gives you clues when you need them. We just need to pay attention. The problem is we are busy paying attention to the judgment of our minds instead of the clues that life is giving us. And then, when the clues of life show up, we question them! We prayed for a clue. The clue shows up. And now we are questioning the clue!

Does this sound familiar?

What would happen if the next time you felt an intuition to pick up the phone and call someone, you just did it? The next time you felt the impulse to go somewhere, you just trusted and went? The next time you sensed that your plan needed to change, you listened without questioning? Without the need to know the outcome, or why?

You think you need to know why. But that isn't your responsibility. Your responsibility is to listen, and act. It's simple.

Because often when you think you know, you really don't.

You end up complicating things with your demands for understanding. If you're not careful, you can be too smart for your own good, constantly questioning and doubting. Your mind seeking to understand before it takes action gets in the way of miracles.

We must learn to develop the courage to act on our deep knowing, instead of constantly filtering. We must learn to trust our guidance instead of interfering. The more you listen, the more you act on it, the more that muscle grows. The more you cultivate your intuition, the more your inner wisdom will guide you. The more your inner wisdom guides you, the more authentically you can live.

Today, whenever I'm trying to figure out where I should go and what I should do, I remember those yellow arrows. I remember the guidance that is all around. All I need to do is follow it.

Think about the GPS on your phone or in your car. You enter your desired destination and then you follow the directions. There is no need to stress or worry. You just listen and you follow. You trust that Siri's got it handled.

Isn't it interesting that we trust Siri more than the universe? We trust Siri more than life.

Now, I don't know about you, but there are times that I question Siri. There are times I think I know better than my GPS. I'll be driving along, following the directions, and then see her instructions, and think: *What is she doing? This GPS doesn't know anything. I'm going to take charge and navigate myself!* Then I go rogue and start making up my own directions, thinking I know better. Maybe I've been there before.

But more often than not, I end up hitting a dead end, or getting stuck in traffic, and it ends up taking longer. Then I'll realize my mistake. Plug Siri back in. And actually surrender.

Why do we trust the GPS? Because it is connected to satellite information that is up to speed on current traffic conditions, road closures, and detours that I can't access with my mind.

But I want you to consider that you, too, have an innate GPS. No, not to traffic patterns but to help guide you with your life. And to fulfill your soul's destiny. It's just that we have stopped listening to our inner guidance. We override it and do our own thing, all the time.

Throughout this journey of surrender, we have learned to surrender attachment to ego, which is always trying to force its own plans. We have surrendered the lies, and gotten in touch with truth, so we can set our coordinates correctly. We've surrendered the illusion of control, so that we can flow with life and be open to where it might be taking us.

Now let's surrender to life's guidance so that we can access more miracles. Because we no longer have to be the one making it all happen, but know that our part is to just be open, available, and act on our guidance.

ONE STEP AT A TIME

Okay, you may be saying, how exactly do you do this, Kute? It seems like a lovely concept, but what if there is no guidance, no clue, no instructions coming in?

There is always a clue. And it isn't outside of you.

The guidance comes from within.

It comes in the form of our intuition.

Intuition arises from the most unconditioned part of us. Not from the ego, but from the deepest dimension of us, the soul. The part of us that always knows what is truly right. So to follow the guidance is a beautiful dance between letting life lead you, and listening within.

I decided, in the writing of this book, to put this theory to the test and take myself on a surrender road trip. I had just returned from one of my Boundless Bliss

Bali events and then spent a couple of days in Ghana with my father for the Christmas holiday. I flew back to Los Angeles on the morning of December twenty-seventh with no plans. I could go back to my home in L.A. or I could travel anywhere in the world.

I stood, ready, at the airport, my bag packed, my spirit willing. Waiting for guidance. I wanted to see what would happen if I totally surrendered completely. What would happen? If I kept saying yes, no matter what. Would it lead me into disaster? Or something magical? If I'm going to write about it, I better make sure this thing works.

In my mind, I was thinking about a few different options. *I could go to Peru, Brazil, the Philippines, Australia.*

But I didn't feel an intuition that any of those choices was right. That "feeling" wasn't there. And I have learned that if you don't feel deep, internal alignment, don't act. Don't force. Be still. Wait and remain open.

Other guidance will arrive.

Now, to wait for guidance doesn't mean you sit at home on your couch, doing nothing. Sometimes you need to ask around. I couldn't simply stand there in the terminal and do nothing. I had to take some preliminary steps. Take a step and look for alignment. Make sure your GPS isn't saying that dreaded "rerouting. . . ."

I walked up to the counter at Philippine Airlines. "When is your next flight to Manila?" I asked.

"Eleven-thirty this evening. We still have seats available. Would you like to purchase one?"

I paused. Checked in. Wasn't feeling it. "Thanks, but I don't think that works for me."

I wandered over to Qantas. They had a flight to Brisbane that left in a few hours.

But it too didn't feel right.

Went to China Airlines. Flight to Beijing at 11:45. "Would you like a ticket?"

No, thank you.

I'm sure people thought I was crazy. Who shows up at the airport with no plans for where they are going to go?

Time was ticking by. If I was going to fly somewhere tonight, I had to make a decision.

I saw the sign for Thai Airways. I walked up to the counter.

The employee looked up with a smile. "Yes, sir, do you have a ticket?"

"Not yet."

"Where do you want to go?"

"I don't know," I said with a laugh.

She looked at me, confused. "We have a flight to Thailand leaving tonight."

I don't want to go to Thailand, I thought.

She continued, "The ticket would cost six hundred dollars."

And despite my mind not wanting to go, I felt deep inside—*Catch this flight.*

Okay. Time for action. I didn't understand why I would be going to Thailand, since I'd been there many times before, but my surrender exercise was to follow the guidance without question.

As I gave her my credit card and walked to the gate, I realized that, even in my attempt to surrender, I was still trying to figure it all out. I decided then and there: *I won't try to understand anything. I will have zero plans for the next six days. Each moment I will listen, surrender, be open, and let life show me what to do next.*

Now, I know that you may not have an open schedule and the funds to travel anywhere in the world your soul guides you to go.

I don't share this story to encourage you to save up for your own surrender road trip. It's not about that. It's about the process of tuning in, listening, and trusting that our internal guidance can be used in our everyday life: in deciding what to do with your day, where to eat dinner, when to change jobs, whether to exercise, when to get out of a relationship, whether to go on a date with that person, whether to invest money in this business or stock.

The problem is we've got to get comfortable making room for stillness. This is where our intuition speaks. In our culture today, we are so intent on being busy and running around, doing, that we've lost touch with simply being. We sometimes think being is not productive.

But sometimes being still is exactly the action that is needed.

Sometimes being still is the most productive thing we can do. When we are still, we allow things to come to us.

The problem is, our ego gets anxious when it doesn't know what is happening. The ego hates stillness. It is uncomfortable with the unknown. In order to try to re-gain control and find "answers," it will manufacture plans that help you feel in "control" but end up taking you way off course. You get into a relationship that you know isn't right. You take a job that isn't quite what you want be-cause it is too uncomfortable waiting for the right one.

You go to a party to fill your calendar because you don't have any other plans and sometimes being alone is uncomfortable.

When we override our intuition, we are reacting. Instead of listening.

In order to surrender to the guidance, we've got to be willing to be still.

Sometimes being in such motion and movement and going so fast, we miss the blessing that is available to us right now because we are running from here to there. But if we are willing to stand still, be still, we allow life to synchronize and fall into place.

So when things seem to not be working in your life, when you've tried and you've pushed, and still hit a wall, consider that this may be a moment to stand still. To tune in. And listen.

The universe is trying to speak to you. Then your blessings may start flowing again.

THE GIFTS OF SURRENDER

When I landed in Thailand twenty hours later, a place that I had been to so many times already, and I didn't really want to be, I got off the plane and stood at the gate. Once again, waiting for guidance. Where do I go now? Maybe someplace I've never been before?

Where would life guide me? Vietnam? Laos? Burma?

And the only message I received was: Bali.

What? I thought. *I literally got back from Bali ten days ago. Why on earth would I go to Bali again?*

But I promised I wasn't going to let my mind guide me this time. I wasn't going to interfere. My internal guidance said Bali. Okay. So I found a ticket counter, bought a flight to Bali, and arrived later that day.

When my driver picked me up at the airport, he said, "What are you doing back here?"

And I looked at him with a smile, and said, "I don't know."

I didn't know and I didn't have to know.

That is the beauty of surrender. Giving up your need to know everything.

The next morning, I headed to one of my favorite restaurants for breakfast. But as I was about to open the door, I felt my guidance say no.

Okay. Inner guidance says don't do what you typically do. So I turned around and looked for other options. I was hungry. I needed to eat.

I was guided to a vegan restaurant down the street, even though it wasn't particularly where I wanted to go.

But I didn't let my mind override. *I don't need to know why. Just follow.* I walked in and they had just two tables available, one for six people, and one for two. They sat me at the one for six people.

I looked around. Didn't they see that I was here by myself?

But I just let it be. I trusted that I was being seated exactly where I needed to be.

I sat down, ordered some food. I said to the universe: *I'm not going to move from this table until some answers come. Universe, I'm here. I'm waiting. What do you have planned?*

I got out my journal and began to write.

Thirty minutes later, I looked up from my journal. And in walked a man who, fifteen years ago, I desperately wanted to meet.

I was in absolute shock.

He was a famous media mogul, and back when I was pitching a television show, I thought he was the key to making it happen. That if I met with him, we would end up working together.

We both lived in L.A. and had never crossed paths despite all my attempts. And yet somehow, of all places, in the middle of nowhere in Bali, on New Year's Day, in he walks.

As he and his companion looked around for a table, there were none available. He walked out.

But his friend looked around and then walked up to me. "Do you mind if my friend and I sit here to eat?"

"Not at all," I said with a smile.

She went outside to gather her friend and they sat down with me, and we began to talk.

Inside of myself, I wanted to burst out laughing at the universe and its plans. *Surrender really works*, I thought. It was like a mini-miracle. Something I had tried to make happen, something I had prayed for, dreamed about, desired for so many years. And then, I let it go. Didn't even want it anymore. And here it was, right in front of me, the universe had brought him to my table to sit right next to me.

This was surrender.

When you let go, you make space for things to happen.

We sat and talked for hours, about life, the ups and downs, success and spirituality.

When he got up to leave, he gave me his phone number and asked for mine. A few minutes later, after he left, I received a text: *Great to meet you. We will do things together. It's God's plan.*

I stared at my phone, the very proof of surrender right in front of me.

Surrender has shown me, time and time again, that I don't have to make it all happen. That when I get myself—my mind, my doubts, my second guessing, my interference—out of the way, life will lead me perfectly to where I need to be. That the universe has its own timing.

I wouldn't say I'm special. We all have this internal guidance. We've just tuned it out.

It's time to tune back in.

LISTENING WITHIN

The more you allow yourself to be open and follow your inner guidance, the more magic will show up in your life.

Take Tyler Perry, one of the most unexpected media moguls in the world and someone whose career has inspired me greatly.

He was born in New Orleans, to a mother who loved

him well, and a father who beat him regularly. When he was young, he saw an episode of *Oprah* on how writing about challenging experiences could lead to personal breakthroughs. Not wanting people to know what he had gone through, which included sexual abuse from multiple people, he wrote about his experiences using different characters. One day, a friend stumbled upon them, and said, "Wow, this is a really good play."

And he decided maybe he should do something with it.

He didn't graduate from high school. He moved to Atlanta, working multiple jobs to save up and put on his first play. He saved twelve thousand dollars, and staged his first production of *I Know I've Been Changed*, about adult survivors of child abuse. Thirty people showed up.

But he didn't give up. "There was something in me that said: This is what you are supposed to do."[1] So he kept going. He tweaked the play, and saved up money again. Put it on again. No one showed up.

He kept doing this for six more years. During this time, he ran out of money several times. Had to sleep out of his car.

How many of us would have given up by this time?

Finally, in 1998, he was about to throw in the towel

and do something else. Something that would actually pay the bills. He thought he was about to put on the final performance.

Right before the show, he looked out the window.

And people were lined up around the block. He had to look twice to make sure his eyes weren't playing tricks on him.

He played to a packed house that night, and received rave reviews. The show went on the road, he began to write new productions, and one day debuted a character that would change the arc of his career: Madea.

The Madea plays became a huge success, and the first film in the franchise, released in 2005, made $50 million.

In 2011, just six years later, *Forbes* listed him as the highest-paid man in entertainment, earning $130 million that year alone. Perry credits the course of his life to miracles. "I know, without a doubt, that what I was experiencing . . . is the essence, power and Grace of God. There is no other explanation for the ways in which my life has unfolded."[2]

Every time he was about to lose faith and give up on his dream, there would be a sign, a message to keep going. "I'd really gotten to the point of thinking this is never going to work. But every time I thought that, there was someone else who'd come along and help my dream find new life."[3]

Tyler Perry worked hard. He believed in his dream. He had so much to overcome. He wasn't a Hollywood insider. He was different, telling stories that were not necessarily valued by the Hollywood establishment. But he knew in his heart the importance of his community and the power in these stories, of strong women like his mother. His intuition told him there was a market. And he was right.

This voice is what kept him going. This is the voice that I'm encouraging you all to listen to. You can call it your gut, your intuition, your inner wisdom, God, your soul. Whatever you want to call it is fine. But just know, it is something that is beyond your mind.

"I call it my God voice. I listen to God through that voice. It's difficult to hear sometimes when things are so crowded and busy. I have to make sure I center myself, especially when I need clarity or answers about the next thing I'm supposed to do. . . . Emotion aside, just get in a clear, quiet place and see how I feel about it. If it feels right I'll move forward. And every time I've gone against that, I've ended up in a bad situation."[4]

This voice has guided him to build his own production studios outside of Atlanta. Has led to a multiyear partnership with Viacom. A career as a writer, actor, director, and producer. And today his net worth is $600 million.

Some would say a miraculous career.

It seemed impossible. But he believed. He listened to the voice within. Didn't question. Didn't just look at the facts, or let his fate limit his destiny. He kept trusting his inner guidance. Looked for the signs. And took action.

This is what it takes.

We often try to overcomplicate it.

When miracles are as natural as the air that we breathe.

Open to the miracles.

Listen for guidance.

Get yourself out of the way.

And follow.

Life will give you more than you thought possible.

Miracles are available to you all the time.

Are you available to them?

CHAPTER FIVE

YOU WERE MADE FOR MORE

PURPOSE

WHAT IF EVERYTHING you've been told about finding your purpose was a myth?

What if seeking your purpose was actually an avoidance of it? Your ego's sneaky way to put off living it, right now?

What if, in fact, there was no need to wait? And waiting was the lie?

I know you have picked up this book because you want to make a difference. Deep inside you, you feel a desire to do more, be more, serve more.

Don't worry. This is what you were made for. It can't not happen, if you truly surrender.

But when we mistakenly think our purpose is this elusive thing out there, to discover and then do, we often end up not living it.

Purpose isn't something you need to find.

It will find you.

So, here's what you need to know.

You. Don't. Need. To. Know.

Let me repeat: You don't need to know your exact life's purpose in order to live it.

How your purpose manifests through you will grow and change as you evolve. It is not some static thing.

So stop trying to find it. Purpose isn't something that you do.

It is who you are being. It is who you are becoming. Moment to moment.

Your purpose is every moment of your life.

Consider that this very moment is your purpose. Now. Now. And now.

When you embrace this, you will begin to experience the magic and the growth that is available in every moment. In every situation. In every day.

WHEN THE WORLD STANDS STILL

During the writing of this book, the world is learning a major lesson in surrender.

As a humanity, we are facing COVID-19 and the world is literally shutting down.

Events were canceled. School was postponed. Nonessential businesses had to close.

Then, we were ordered by our governments to stay in our homes. Social distancing, a term we had never heard of before, became a way of life.

We have no choice. It is for the salvation of humanity.

I'm sure everyone had great plans for 2020. As I write this, they are now all up in the air.

It is a time of great uncertainty and fear.

But also, opportunity.

Now, I know it has been devastating for many. Paychecks that people depend on have disappeared. People are getting laid off. Loved ones are fearful for their health. Our economy is in turmoil. So many people have died.

And yet somehow, when I look around, at the deeper level of what's going on, I can't help but see it as the universe inviting us to change.

There is something deeper seeking to emerge from this emergency.

It is forcing us to slow down. To be still. Focus on our

families. Remember what is truly important in our lives. What is essential.

To go inside ourselves and listen more deeply to our souls. To go outside and take in nature. To appreciate all the things we took for granted in our lives. The simple things. Things we never seemed to have time for, we somehow now have time for.

It is a reset for all of humanity.

Did you know the Chinese word for crisis also means opportunity?

If this very moment is indeed our purpose, then this situation isn't something to suffer through, a punishment to wait out. It could be the greatest growth opportunity of our lives.

We are being called to evolve. It feels like we are in a process of purification.

We are being invited to make a shift: from the ego-centric way of living—*me me me*—to one of cooperation, connectivity, and soul-centeredness. Our future depends on it.

We are being forced to question the kind of world we want to create moving forward. Because the way we've been doing things up to now clearly hasn't worked.

We have literally been forced by the universe to

unplug from the hustle and bustle of life and listen to our deepest truth.

It is a process of global surrender.

I know it is hard for many to feel like we are stuck on pause. All our intended plans! It is hard not to feel powerless. We judge ourselves for not being as productive. We can't see anyone or go anywhere, thinking, *This is such a waste of time!*

But if we truly know why we are here, it is not.

So, are you ready to learn your true purpose? I know you've been seeking. I know you want to find it. You think it looks different for each person, so you are out there looking for your own unique, fingerprinted purpose.

But I'm here to tell you: We are not so different, you and I.

Our purpose is one and the same for each person on this planet.

We are here to grow and evolve.

That's it. Plain and simple.

It isn't about being Gandhi or Mother Teresa. It isn't just about saving the world, feeding the hungry, creating a cure. Yes, those things are important and are sometimes the work we are called to do. But our true purpose isn't at the surface level. It is at the soul level. And ultimately, the purpose of the soul is to evolve.

What matters is not simply what we do, but who we become in the process of life itself.

RESET

I talked to a friend during the lockdown who was struggling with the restrictions of the quarantine, fighting his isolation and his inability to be productive. I asked him what he did with his week. And he said: "Well, I procrastinated a ton, organized my closet, but I also finally had some very difficult conversations with my parents that I'd been hoping to have for many years. It was so healing and very powerful."

Given the social isolation, he'd taken the time to pick up the phone and call his parents, something he rarely did in his everyday life. He then went on to tell me about the very transformative conversations that had taken place. He'd finally spoken his truth to them. Stood up for himself, and shared some feelings that he had been holding back for years.

As I listened to him talk, he was judging himself harshly about not getting as much work done as he thought he should have, when in truth, he had managed to get the most important work done. He had taken this time to do what I call *soul work*. He had conversations that allowed him to release past pain and resentments. So that he could grow and evolve. He had freed himself from a burden that he'd been carrying for many years.

You see, we need to have a deeper understanding of productivity. I'm not saying that we should all sit in our houses on meditation cushions for the rest of our lives. No. When we grow and evolve as a soul, it frees up our energy and often propels us into action. When we are in tune with our purpose on the inside, it will only lead us more quickly to our purpose on the outside.

But we must start with the internal. Even if you have your dream job, and are out there doing what you think you need to be doing, if you aren't growing and learning the lessons your soul is here for, it will not truly fulfill you. There are people who seemed to be doing exactly what they were born to do, and yet they lived incredibly unhappy lives. Elvis Presley. Anthony Bourdain. Vincent van Gogh.

So let me be clear. Purpose isn't simply something we go out to find. It is first and foremost who we are being, how we are growing, what we are learning, in every moment of our lives.

The ego says: I'm going to find my purpose.

The soul knows: This very moment is my purpose.

You, dear reader, are in the classroom of life.

CLASS IS IN SESSION

If the purpose of our lives is to grow and evolve, then everyone is your teacher.

The boss you hate.

The jerk who cut you off in traffic.

Your child who tries your patience daily.

The ex who knows exactly how to push your buttons.

They were not placed in your life randomly. They are here for a reason. They are your coursework, your curriculum, your lesson plan, and your test.

Yes, you can resist them. You can fight them. You can judge them. But then you will only suffer. And you will miss out.

Or you can surrender to the purpose that they are serving, and see what lessons they are here to teach you. Who they are inviting you to become.

Sometimes the lessons are subtle.

Sometimes they smack you in the face.

But until you face them fully, and surrender to the process they are inviting you toward—to learn forgiveness, to stand up for yourself, to take responsibility—you'll stay stuck in this pattern. You will keep bringing back the same situations in your life until you have learned the lesson.

It is only then that you will graduate and experience something new.

When you learn the lesson, that's what unlocks the door to the next level of your life.

If you don't learn it, you repeat the same lesson. Over and over. Like *Groundhog Day*.

One of the lessons in my particular soul curriculum is patience. Everything seems to take me a bit longer, from landing my first girlfriend, to building my business. Until I realized this was actually my soul's lesson plan, I found myself getting frustrated. *Why do things always seem to take me so long? Why can't for once in my life things go smoothly? Why is it so easy for others?*

But once I started to connect the dots, see the patterns, and understand my soul's lesson plan, then, when situations arise that test me, rather than getting reactive and irritated, I'm able to take a step back and realize: *Oh, I'm in the classroom of patience right now.* Instead of resisting, I look for how the situation is inviting me to grow.

I remember that life is my classroom, and this very moment is my purpose. What is it trying to teach me?

What is the lesson my soul needs to learn?

Life will give you clues as to what your lessons are. There will be certain patterns in your life that you cannot deny. Do you often find yourself with overbearing bosses? Maybe you are here to learn to stand up for yourself. Do you constantly get into relationships with partners who cheat? Maybe you are here to learn to value your self-worth. Do you seem to attract competitive friendships, people who stab you in the back instead of supporting you? Maybe you need to look at your past and make amends with someone you betrayed.

Consider how these very patterns, that you've long resisted, could be trying to serve you. Could be inviting you to grow, evolve, heal, and become more of who you are meant to be.

Now, let me be clear. I'm not saying stay in an abusive situation. But sometimes to learn the lesson is to look the situation straight in the face. Sometimes to surrender is not to back down, but to stand up and face your demons. Sometimes surrender is not to run away, but to stay in the fire and learn the lesson once and for all. To surrender to the situation as it stands today. So you can notice red flags earlier next time. Love yourself fully. Understand your worth. And attract something different going forward.

It might sound counterintuitive to stay in the situation and learn what you need to learn. But otherwise, you'll attract something else to teach you the same lesson down the road. Different person, different situation, but same issue, same pattern, same curriculum. Ultimately the common denominator is you. And you can't run away from yourself. You cannot escape the lesson.

The perspective from which you view each situation in your life is how you will experience each situation. You can see it as a tragedy that is happening to you, and stay stuck in victim mode, asking *why* is this happening to me?

Or you can see it as a lesson plan, an opportunity, asking why *is* this happening?

Same question. Different perspective.

One is ego. One is soul.

I know this isn't always easy. It isn't what we have been taught.

But if this is our true purpose, then each situation that you've faced in your life has been orchestrated for your growth.

MAKING PEACE WITH THE PAST

I remember when I was eight years old. My father used to call me up onstage to give a sermon at church, with no preparation, no warning at all. Imagine, sitting in the crowd, dreaming about soccer, when you hear your name. Your father is up onstage, looking at you, waiting for you to take your place at the podium. You walk up slowly and turn toward the congregation, the bright lights blinding you, the silence deafening. You have no idea what to say.

But as much as I disliked those moments as a child, I have to say, they certainly prepared me for my life today.

I could be half asleep, and if someone said, "Come up onstage. We need you to speak!" I would be ready. I don't have to have things planned. I don't feel like it is me who does the speaking anyway. Something takes over me when I speak.

So even though I didn't technically follow in my

father's footsteps by taking over his churches, I certainly followed his path in a different way, and being his son was the perfect preparation for the way my life would unfold, as much as I sometimes hated it at the time.

So consider: What if everything in your life was preparation for your purpose? What if everything that happened in your life was setting the stage for who you are to become?

Once you realize that life is a school, and every experience a lesson plan, then it helps you to make peace with the pain of your past. You understand it wasn't a punishment. You start looking for how it serves the reason for why you are alive on this planet. It was the universe preparing you for what you are here to do. Your bankruptcy, your divorce, your heartbreak, the death of your parents. The universe is using all of it to get you ready.

There is power in asking: How did these experiences serve me? How have these experiences been preparing me to give my gifts?

Sometimes when we are still resisting what has happened, because we haven't seen the soul lesson, then it is hard to embrace the purpose. So we can't surrender to the gift it is trying to give us.

But if our past weren't what it was, we wouldn't be

where we are today. And we certainly wouldn't be what we're going to be tomorrow.

I know that it can be hard to make peace with the pain. But making peace with the pain will bless you.

There is a freedom that becomes available once you can make peace with your past. This doesn't mean that you don't feel sadness. That you don't grieve. That you aren't angry about what happened. No. Feelings must be felt fully, and acknowledged. Feel it fully. But once the time of heartbreak has passed, it is time to look back with courage, and surrender your pain and hurt.

When we can surrender to our past, and thank our past, then the gift of the experience can release itself to us. When you resist, the gift remains trapped. When you embrace it, as a necessary part of your soul's curriculum, the gift gets activated. This is the magic. We say thank you, and we focus on the lessons, and the learning.

Thank it for preparing you for this moment.

Thank it for shaping you into the person you are today.

Yes, that means saying thank you for the heartache, the heartbreak, the loss, the death. All of it.

Sometimes we are not ready to do that.

But nothing will change the fact that what has happened, has happened. Whether you surrender or not, it has already happened. Your holding on will not change the past. It only blocks your moving toward your future.

When we surrender to what is, what has happened, loss can be transformed. Because you didn't really lose, you only gained, if you learned the lesson.

ACTIVATING THE GIFT

When my mother passed away, I was heartbroken. I felt like my life was just beginning. I had just achieved the success I'd always dreamed of, I no longer needed to hustle so much, thus I felt like I finally had the bandwidth to be able to spend more time with her, and then she died.

I didn't understand.

Deep down, I'd always thought my father would die first. He's ten years older than my mother. It would only make sense. And I thought his death would prepare me for hers.

And now everything was backward. It wasn't supposed to happen this way.

But soon after my mother's death, I felt her presence.

I felt her telling me: *I'm giving you this gift. I know we have been so close all these years. But you need to fully heal your relationship with your father. It is time. You don't know when he will go. Don't take the opportunity you have now for granted.*

My father and I did not have the closest relationship when I was a child. He was always traveling or focused on the church. I don't recall him ever attending any school event or game. For many years, I carried around this pain in regard to my father. The story in my mind was that I wasn't important to him.

My mother's death was an invitation to learn a lesson.

Sure, I could have stayed a victim, angry, and not taken advantage of the opportunity I was being given.

But I'm happy to say that I got the soul purpose perspective. I didn't want my mother to have died in vain.

I made a choice to live my purpose. Today, I visit him in Ghana every few months. I call him every day. The only days I don't call him are when I'm on a plane and it just isn't possible. All the other days, I call my father. It is my duty, my devotion, my privilege. I made a decision to just love him, fully, every day that I have left with him.

I decided there was more freedom if I would surrender to the lesson. Be right, and not have a relationship with my father? Or realize that there is no time to waste? And all that matters is the loving. Which was healing for both of us. I am making up for thirty years with my father right now. I don't know how much more time we have left. But I promised myself I will have no regrets when he dies.

This is a gift from my mother.

Should my mother not have died? Should that bad thing not have happened? But in that so-called bad thing happening, was it bad? Or was it a blessing? What is bad? What is good? Had she stayed alive, this profound healing would not have happened between my father and me.

She gave me, in her passing, the gift of this new relationship with my father. Now I am able to thank the universe for her death and see it as a blessing. Because I see how it changed my life, helped me evolve and grow as a son.

There is power in thanking your past. Because even all the ways that my father wasn't there for me made me who I am today. So the good, the bad, the beautiful, and the ugly. All of it led you here. To today. To this moment. To this opportunity.

So, what if you blessed your past today?

Thank you, parents. Even though you were different
    than I wanted you to be, I see now that you were
    the perfect parents for me, in this life.
Thank you.
Thank you to my ex. Even though you broke my heart,
    and caused me so much pain, I see now that you
    were the one who mirrored to me my own relation-
    ship with myself and forced me to own my own
    worth.
Thank you, pain.
Thank you, abuse.
Thank you, loss.
Thank you, tragedy.
Thank you, poverty.
Thank you, divorce.
I know I resisted you in the moment. I know that I
    wish there had been another way.
But thank you. For what you are here to teach me.
I will no longer resist.

I will embrace. I will surrender. So I open to my bless-
    ing and receive the gift.
Thank you.

It's not just what you *think* about that creates your reality, it's what you *thank* about.

When you can see that the challenges, the hardships, the ups and the downs, the divorces and the break-ups, are just life's way of preparing your soul, everything shifts. They were preparation: sculpting you to develop the resilience to become the person you were meant to be.

Everything is working together for your good.

Everything is in service to your evolution.

FROM PAIN TO PURPOSE

Do you know about Malala Yousafzai?

Malala was eleven years old when the Taliban took control of her town in Pakistan. They said girls were no longer allowed to go to school. Malala loved school more than anything. She and her father, a schoolteacher, began to speak out. They described to media outlets what it was like to live under Taliban rule, and argued that girls had the right to an education.

Malala soon began to take the bus to a school in another town, defying the Taliban's orders.

A few years later, when she was fifteen years old, on her way home from school, a masked man boarded the school bus with a gun in his hand.

He turned to the girls, who were shaking in their seats. "Who is Malala?" he asked.

Malala raised her hand. And he shot her in the side of the head.

She woke up ten days later in a hospital in England.

The fact that Malala survived the shooting is nothing short of a miracle.

Now, in the moment, when a young girl is shot in the face on the way home from school, it is hard not to think: What a tragedy. How could this be happening?

But today, when you look back on what has transpired since that fateful day, it is hard not to see purpose in that pain.

That incident transformed Malala from a girl pursuing an education into an icon and symbol of courage and bravery. As this young girl healed, and fought to be able to walk again, and speak again, and live again, she did not back down but came back stronger.

"When you . . . are nearly killed, and after that you survive and you are alive and still speaking out, then there is nothing else you should be afraid of. . . . What else can they do? They can only kill me. And it didn't work. So it means nothing else can work. And this movement is still alive . . . this voice, it's still alive . . . I believe and I know for sure that if you have strong commitment within your heart, if you have love in your heart, that you want to do something better, the whole world and the whole universe supports you and your cause."[1]

Malala says she never had a "why me" moment. That if she'd gotten stuck in "why me," nothing would have been done. She knows that she was chosen for this miracle, that it was not random, and she feels called to give her entire life to this cause.

This is surrender.

Two years after the shooting, Malala was the youngest ever recipient of the Nobel Peace Prize, at age seventeen. Today she has spoken at the United Nations, appeared on countless television shows, written a *New*

York Times best seller, and appeared in an acclaimed documentary. Her Malala Fund raises millions of dollars to help the more than 130 million girls who remain without access to education.

She harbors no bitterness. She is not angry. She is convicted of her purpose and will go forward, each day, doing what she can to change that situation.

"People prayed to God to spare me, and I was spared for a reason—to use my life for helping people."[2]

This is what it means to understand your purpose. You know that every moment of your life has been preparing you for this. This calling. This crisis. This moment in time.

ONE SMALL STEP

Now, Malala didn't grow up thinking that she had to craft her purpose, create it out of thin air. She had no master plan, no vision board with pictures of a Nobel Prize. She just started where she was. Just went in a direction that she was guided. Stood up for what she believed in. And unfortunately, those actions got her shot.

But was it fortunate or unfortunate that she was shot? It depends on what lens you are looking through. From the ego, of course, it is bad. But from the soul purpose perspective, it's not good. It's perfect.

Imagine if Malala wasn't shot in the head. Would any of us know who she is right now?

Malala didn't plan it all out. She just started. She looked at her life to see what it was preparing her for. And then took the next step. Speak out against the Taliban. Take a bus to school. Then, after the shooting, work to be able to walk again. Strive to be able to speak again. Once her voice returned, she had no question as to what she would use it for. It was obvious.

We don't have to start off with some epic plan for our purpose. This is a myth. Just the ego's illusion. You can simply take the next step and go in the direction that your soul is nudging you. Your purpose is not something you need to figure out, like a complicated math equation; it is a humble, daily revelation that emerges in the process of living life itself.

When you take a step, no matter how small, life reveals what's next.

Take another step, and life continues to reveal.

Many times there is something more that is seeking to be expressed through us and we have to give up our ego's idea of what we think our purpose is so that we can open to something more. This allows us to be used in a bigger way than we have prepared for, or could imagine. We must be willing to surrender the attachment to *I really want my purpose to be this.*

Malala didn't know she was going to be Malala. That's the magic! There is no way she could have architected being Malala. It just happened because she was evolving and going in the direction of her soul's guidance, which placed her on the bus at that particular time.

We don't know what our Malala moment will be. We don't have to know.

We just have to be willing to show up and respond to the authentic call in the moment. And show up, doing the best we can, every moment of our lives.

That's when the magic of surrender can happen and our purpose can unfold.

What this lens does is allow you to give up the wait. You are no longer waiting to figure out what your purpose is, you are no longer holding out until you find the right job, until you retire, until you get enough money, until you find the perfect relationship. So long as you are using every moment to evolve, to heal, to transform, to contribute, then essentially, you are living the purpose for your existence in every moment. Then waiting stops and life takes on a different quality.

The truth is not everyone is meant to be Nelson Mandela, jailed for twenty-seven years. That doesn't make your purpose less important, less epic, or less worthy. We don't need a bunch of Gandhis, or Martin Luther King Jr.'s walking around. I share their wisdom in this book because they can show us what it means to be surrendered. But what the world needs is you being 100 percent you, available to life, every single day. Tapped into who you are meant to be. That is when your purpose will find you. And that is the greatest gift you can give the world.

The only thing that is blocking us from our purpose is our big plans. Because we are so busy trying to do something big that many times we don't even start. For our ego, it is either too overwhelming that we don't know how we are going to do it, or we think it isn't important enough so we don't start. And then nothing happens.

Malala started small.

She got on the bus.

Many of us don't get on the bus because we think we should be flying on a jumbo jet instead. But we've got to get on the bus. Look where getting on the bus led her.

Look where refusing to get off the bus led Rosa Parks. Look where standing outside of the embassy led Greta Thunberg.

These were seemingly small moments. Which led to big change.

There is no need to wait. This very moment is it.

Look for the lessons. Learn the lessons. Grow. And evolve. Then as you grow and evolve, your purpose will grow and change with you.

Purpose is revealed through you in direct proportion to the evolution of your soul. Your purpose is not a fixed thing but will become bigger and greater as you become more of who you are meant to be.

The secret to greatness is not some far-off thing, for the select few. They were not born that way, in some genetic lottery.

No. Greatness is an invitation.

Greatness is what you are.

Greatness is your willingness to stop waiting and instead respond to its call.

CHAPTER SIX

THE ULTIMATE LETTING GO

LOVE

STOP SEEKING LOVE. You won't find it that way.

How do you find something that isn't even lost?

The more you chase, the more it eludes you.

Haven't you realized?

Love isn't what you've been taught.

Love is not a fleeting feeling.

Love is not a mere emotion.

Love is not a fairy-tale fantasy, a happily-ever-after guarantee.

Love is not about getting. Fill me up. Make me feel worthy.

It's not something you deserve only if you behave the right way.

It's not something you receive as part of a trade.

It is time to surrender to the love that you are.

And love fully, with nothing held back.

This is our calling. This is our destiny. This is the ultimate surrender.

We are love. And to share love with the world is the most powerful thing you can do.

To be great does not have to mean that you go out and build a successful company. To be great does not mean that you are famous with millions of followers. To be great doesn't require a ton of money in your bank account.

You might have all of those things. But they don't make you great.

To be great means that you love, fully, in this life. And the fruit of that love is what changes the world.

LOVESICK

It's only when we surrender our false ideas of love that we can embrace our calling.

Mom loves you. *But be a good girl.*

I love you. *But only if you love me the way I expect to be loved.*

God loves you. *But if you don't follow his rules, there are some serious consequences for eternity!*

Does this sound like real love to you?

When we think this is love, we tend to get desperate for it. Then much of what we do, we do in the frantic search for love. Even the drive for success, money, fame, and power is, underneath it all, the need to be loved.

When we mistakenly think love is conditional, we hold it back. We wait to love until someone behaves the way we want, gives us what we need, in order to deserve our love.

Once you find the one, you'll be complete. Without your lover, you're nothing. These ideas pervade our society and culture. Think about Trisha Yearwood's "How Do I Live Without You?" or *Romeo and Juliet*. Think about *Jerry Maguire*, pretty much every romantic comedy ever made—in fact, every movie ever made! The kind of love Hollywood presents is: *If I need you, and you need me, that's love.*

They've turned love into a drug. We need it. We crave it. We wither away without it.

That's not love. That is codependency.

When you buy into that version of love, then you can be sold.

You are not enough.

So you need this lipstick, to be desirable.

So if you drive this car, you'll be worthy

If you wear these clothes, you'll be accepted.

This idea of love feeds on the consumerist mindset and keeps our economy running.

But true love does not have a list of requirements, a combination lock that if someone gets it right, your love can finally be unleashed.

No. True love is freely given. With nothing expected in return. Love is not dependent on external factors.

Love is a choice, an inner moment-by-moment decision, a gift that we can give to anyone, at any time.

OUR TRUE NATURE

I know it may not always feel this way. No matter who you are, you have likely suffered in love. I understand. It is not easy being a human being.

Maybe your parents didn't give you what you needed. They were selfish, bitter, and angry, even abusive. Perhaps they made you feel less-than, unloved, and unworthy.

Maybe with your siblings it was always a competition. You felt like an outsider in your own family, that they were loved more.

Maybe you've been single for years and you feel like a failure. You're tired of searching. You feel like giving up. You can't help thinking: *What's wrong with me?*

Maybe you've been betrayed or cheated on. People have let you down and you just don't believe in love anymore.

I get it. Sometimes those who should love us the most hurt us the most. And so we run from love because we can't face being hurt yet again. We'd rather stay safe than go through another heartbreak. We're not sure we'd survive.

I understand why you might feel this way.

But I want you to know.

You were made to love.

You can't run away from what you are.

To run from what you truly are is the most painful thing you can do. Because if there is one thing we were born to do, it is to love.

Take a moment and consider how we all started in this life. When you look at newborn babies, they are full of love. Love radiates from their being. You could put an infant in front of a criminal and that baby would reach out for his face, smiling, gurgling, seeking to connect, full of love for whoever is in front of them. The love isn't about the other person. It's about who that baby is. They are love, personified.

Love is our true nature. We are here to share it with each and every person we come in contact with.

A baby doesn't reserve its love for only its family members. Babies don't ration out their love to share only with those who love them back.

And yet it is what we learn to do, over time.

Our essential nature gets suppressed through the course of our lives. It starts when our parents, despite their best intentions, didn't know how to love us uncon-ditionally. When we behaved badly, our parents often punished us. Maybe they sent us to our rooms, gave us a certain look of disdain, they yelled, maybe they took away our favorite toy. We interpreted that punishment to mean that we were bad. We learned that if we did the right things, we would be loved. We determined that love isn't something freely given, but something that gets dis-pensed when we exhibit the right behaviors. Get good grades, earn the gold medal, be pretty. Then Daddy loves me.

This is when love becomes conditional.

When we buy into this paradigm, we think we've got to work for love, to earn our worthiness. This belief system becomes so ingrained in us, we don't even realize it is a story we've made up about reality; we think it *is* the reality. So we seek love, out there, forgetting we already have it within us.

We betray our feelings.

We pretend to be people we're not.

We say yes when we mean no.

Just because you are not in touch with the love that you are, doesn't mean you aren't love.

It is the very foundation of your being.

I'm going to show you the freedom that is available when you step off the hamster wheel. When you stop performing, manipulating, and seeking.

And remember who you truly are, and love freely.

UNCONDITIONAL

The other day, I was hiking in the Hollywood Hills with one of my friends. She's constantly complaining to me that her husband isn't affectionate enough; that he doesn't give her what she needs. Today, she told me that she'd had enough. She was now going to withhold her affection in protest, until he started expressing love for her in the ways that she wanted. She'd made a choice to become distant and cold, thinking this was going to change him. Yet this only made her more miserable and unhappy as they grew further and further apart.

As I listened to her justifications for holding back her love, I interrupted her and asked a simple question: "Look, you might be right. I'm not going to argue with you; he isn't the most affectionate man. But do you love him?"

She looked at me, confused, grumbling, "Yes, of course I do. I've been with him fourteen years!"

"So are you going to divorce him?"

"No!"

"Then it's really not that complicated. Complain, groan, and be upset. Or surrender to the opportunity to love him more deeply. Give up the negotiation. Just love him the way you want to be loved, the way you know how to love."

She sighed and considered my suggestion. "But, Kute, he's not loving me the way I want to be loved. It feels one-sided. I keep telling him and he still doesn't do it. Shouldn't love be mutual? Why do I always have to be the one who reaches out, who initiates? It's not fair."

I looked at her with compassion. "You're right, but your 'buts' and protests won't bring you any closer. It won't get you what you want, which is love and connection. I want you to consider that he isn't intentionally withholding the love that you desire. He's not a jerk. You know he's a good man. So maybe he doesn't know *how* to love you the way you want to be loved."

She looked at me intently. She always interpreted his actions as him not loving her and she took it very personally. Maybe it wasn't about her at all.

"Maybe his parents weren't affectionate with each other, they weren't affectionate with him, so you are asking him to speak a language he doesn't really understand. He has no framework for how to love you the way you want to be loved. Maybe your presence in his life is to help him open his heart and learn to love in this way."

We paused at the top of the hill and considered the beautiful Los Angeles vista. I continued: "Maybe showing your husband how to love in this way is why you came together. And presents a healing opportunity for him. Is this a gift you could give him? Just imagine him as a little boy, five years old. No one is loving him. And now he is a grown man, with this fragile five-year-old boy inside him, who has never been loved. Doesn't know how to love. So next time you see him, see the five-year-old boy inside him who is hurting and doesn't even know he is hurting, wants love but never learned how to ask for it or share it. Let that soften your heart and love him more compassionately."

She stared out at the horizon, tears welling in her eyes. She nodded slowly.

"How could you go about loving him, exactly as he is today? With no clauses, no requirements, no need for altered behavior?"

What would love look like if it was truly unconditional? The way it was intended?

Let me be clear. To love unconditionally doesn't necessarily mean we stay in relationships that are unfulfilling. That we betray who we are and our authentic needs in order to keep the other person happy. Or stay in relationships that are physically, mentally, or emotionally abusive. But to love unconditionally is to accept who the other person is, and we no longer require them to be different before we can love them.

Love is no longer a transaction or trade but a choice.

That may mean how they are acting doesn't necessarily work for what you need. And you might need to step away. It may mean you break up with them, or spend less time with them, or get some space for a while. But that doesn't mean the loving has to stop. You can still love them.

Nothing they do has the power to take away your love.

I turned away from the beautiful view as we continued our hike. "One of the reasons my father and I weren't close for many years is that I wanted him to be different than he was. I was caught up in my belief system: *He doesn't call me. He doesn't make any effort. I'm not important to him. A relationship is a two-way street and I can't always be the one making all the effort.*"

She nodded her head. She could relate to those feelings.

"But once my mother died, I realized that I could stay in my righteousness about my position—and end up never having a relationship with my father; or I could just let go and surrender to the fact that I do love him. And actually just *love* him. I asked myself: What would it be like to love my father without conditions? Love him without requirements? Love him without needing him to be any different than he is today? I had this epiphany. If I love him, why not just love him?"

I looked over at my friend with tears in my eyes. I wanted her to realize how much freedom we truly have to love others, exactly as they are. But you have to be more committed to loving than to being right.

"I am happy to say that I chose love. I chose to love my father exactly as he is. And doing that transformed our relationship. The fact is, my father isn't going to change. He is eighty-four years old! And he doesn't need to change. I realized that it doesn't matter if he calls or doesn't call. If I stay hooked into the idea that I'm right, then I would never have a relationship with him, and I would miss out. So I just surrendered it all.

"Surrendered the expectation that he be different.

"Surrendered the idea that he was wrong.

"Surrendered the pattern of holding back my love until he acted the way I wanted him to act.

"I just surrendered. And loved him. Now I call him every day."

My heart swelled with emotion as I remembered how powerfully freeing this choice was. This choice changed everything.

And it can for you too.

People say love hurts. But it isn't love that hurts. It is the limited expectations we place on love that cause us hurt. *If I love you, you have to give it back to me. And then when you don't, I experience pain. If you love me, you need to love me in the way I wasn't loved, and make up for all the ways I wasn't loved growing up.*

That's not love. That's a transaction.

To love unconditionally is what you were made for. But in order to love unconditionally, we have to realize there is no shortage of love. There is no famine, no drought, no bankruptcy.

We have an unlimited supply of love within us. Every time you make a withdrawal, your balance doesn't deplete, it actually grows because you and your loving expand.

You will not lose anything if you love, fully.

It is time to surrender the scarcity mindset that makes you hold back love, and embrace the abundance of love within you.

GROWTH POTION

The other day, a woman at one of my events raised her hand. She said, "Kute, I feel like giving up, like I'm never going to meet my soul mate. Like it is never going to happen. Should I give up?"

With a smile, I responded: "Guess what? I can help you find your soul mate in less than five minutes."

She looked at me in shock, yet eager to hear my secret.

And I said: "Close your eyes and imagine the most challenging person in your life right now. The one you get angry at. The one who frustrates you. The one who annoys you the most. Do you have them in mind?"

She nodded.

"Good news. That's your soul mate."

She looked at me in astonishment. "Kute, what are you talking about?"

"Each and every person you attract into your life is your soul mate. I'm your soul mate. Your siblings are your soul mates. Your parents? Definitely your soul mates! A soul mate isn't necessarily someone whom you stay with forever. A soul mate isn't necessarily some perfect human being who meets your every need and loves you every second of the day. No human can actually live up to that. A soul mate is someone who causes you to see parts of yourself you've long suppressed and invites you to grow. **A soul mate is a mirror. To show you more of yourself.** What would change about your life if you understood who your soul mate truly is?"

She looked at me in agreement.

"Everything," she said in a small voice.

Exactly.

We get sold the story that out there is a soul mate who will complete us. Who will love us in all the ways we weren't loved. Who will make us feel like we are enough. And then, when in romantic relationships we don't feel complete, we don't feel understood, we think something is wrong. And we go off seeking that "perfect" love once again.

This is why we suffer so much in love. Because we misunderstand what it is.

The purpose of relationships is no different than the purpose of life. People are placed in our lives to help us grow and evolve. Every relationship you've ever had, your soul and their soul had an agreement. Consider that they were angels in disguise. Sent to you with a gift that you have the opportunity to unwrap by learning the lesson.

Yes, even the woman who cheated on you. Even the boyfriend you loved so deeply and yet broke your heart.

Sure, you can resist who they were to you, be angry with them, wish they had been different, and miss the lesson. Or you can get curious about why they were a part of your journey.

And become fully receptive to their gift.

Now, this doesn't mean you don't walk away from a relationship that isn't working. But you can reframe what success in a relationship is. Then when issues come up in any relationship, you are able to go through it consciously, with awareness and understanding. *What is the lesson? Can I learn the lesson and then move on? Or is there more growth here for me in this relationship?*

You deserve to be loved well. Don't get me wrong. But when we put conditions on love, and only want it to look a certain way, which is often shaped by unrealistic portrayals of love in the media, we miss out on the real point of love.

Love is that which causes you and all around you to grow the most.

That is love. Love is that which serves your soul's evolution.

Do you see how sometimes that means love isn't comfortable? That love requires growth?

So who do you struggle with the most? Who triggers you? Who frustrates you? Consider that they are bringing parts of you to light that need attention, that need healing. Instead of hating them, look inside yourself. See what they are reflecting to you, about yourself.

Relationships are a mirror. Do you like what you see?

Sometimes your greatest soul mates are those people

who come into your life as a catalyst. Their presence forces you to face emotions that you've suppressed from the past that you have long tried to run from. When you surrender to the reason they have shown up in your life, and then courageously feel and heal those parts of yourself that you've denied, you'll become ripened and ready to truly love more deeply, whether it is with them or someone else.

LIFE LESSON

I remember when I first started giving seminars, when I was twenty years old, I proudly invited my then girlfriend to one, excited for her to see me up onstage.

A few hours into the second day, I looked over to where she'd been sitting and she was gone. Thinking she must have gone to the bathroom, I didn't worry too much about it, until a bit later in the afternoon and I noticed that she still wasn't back.

By the end of the day I was furious. I drove straight over to her apartment, burst through the door to find her sitting calmly on the couch with a book, and said, "What's going on? Why did you leave?"

She set down the book and looked at me with compassion.

"I'm sorry, I knew that it would upset you. But I couldn't stay in that room. I've been telling you for months that I think you have unresolved anger toward your father. I get that you aren't ready to deal with it, but to see you up onstage telling everyone to deal with their issues, when you have clearly not dealt with yours? It just felt inauthentic. I couldn't be there."

I looked at her in shock. I was so offended. Me, inauthentic?

Who did she think she was? What did she know?

I broke up with her on the spot.

What she said about my father? I ignored it. Focused on how wrong she was. Moved on. Relationship over. Goodbye.

A year later, I met the woman with whom I fell deeply in love and was with for four and a half years. And a few months in, guess what she said: "I think you have unresolved anger toward your father."

Oh my God, I couldn't believe it. *Again? Really?*

But this time, I didn't want to sacrifice the relationship. I loved this woman. So I put my ego aside. And realized that maybe there was some truth to what they both were saying. I knew it was time to face myself and deal with my unresolved issues. They were getting in the way of letting me love more fully.

This was the gift.

Love is ultimately a purification. Your true soul mate will cause you to question yourself, become more conscious of your patterns. Sure, it may not always feel great. But it allows you to let go of unnecessary baggage that has been weighing you down, and in doing so, it will allow you to fly and be more free.

Everything changes when you understand that relationships are a transformational portal to the highest version of yourself. Don't just view them based on society's standards, but become aware of their true purpose.

So how do you know when a relationship is over? On one level, it's simple, but it's not always easy. Two people initially come together because they are vibrating at a similar level of energy and consciousness. They have things to teach each other and lessons to learn.

A relationship is about two people going in a similar direction, at a similar pace, with a joint commitment to serving each other. The problem comes when one person is no longer committed to serving the other person's soul, or when one person grows in a totally different direction and leaves the other person behind. Then the relation-ship is over.

Or if you realize that you are no longer growing together, maybe your lessons are complete. Or maybe you've stopped committing to learning the lessons to-gether. Then you have to be honest about that. Maybe you've changed so much since meeting, that your needs, values, and goals have evolved and you are no longer compatible. You have to figure out who you both truly are and see if you can get on the same page again. If so, this is another opportunity for growth, to re-create your relationship. And if not, then sadly, it may be time to move on.

None of this means it is a failure. It just means the reason why you have come together is complete.

So long as you've learned the lesson, you are graduating.

Success in relationships is the degree to which you learn the lesson and become the most authentic version of yourself, individually and as a couple.

Sometimes we confuse a life partner with a life lesson and then suffer when the relationship ends. Even though it served its purpose. It was a success, if you grew as a person. If you changed and became more of who you are meant to be.

FORMLESS

Our society thinks the only way a relationship can be a success is if it lasts forever. This is not true. Don't get so attached to the form.

No form lasts forever. All forms are temporary. Your lovers may leave you. Your kids will grow up and live their own lives. Even if you stay married until your death, one day one of you is going to die. Does that mean your love wasn't valid? Does it mean your love disappears?

No. Your love continues. Remember, love is a state of being. And no one can take it away from you.

So be committed to the loving, not just the form.

We often get attached to the form. If you are going to be attached to anything, be attached to the loving. If you are attached to the loving, then, regardless of the forms, you will live that loving.

One evening, I sat in the garden, outside the house I grew up in in South London. My mother was watering the flowers, enjoying the fresh air. We'd just returned from one of her chemo sessions, and it always helped to get outside afterward.

I was catching up on some email, when I looked up from my phone and saw my mother, with the sun setting just behind her.

"Mama," I said, "let's sit and talk."

She sat down on the bench next to me.

"When I asked you whether you were afraid of dying, you said no. That the soul lives forever and that you want what God wants. But are you really not afraid?"

She tilted her head, considering my question. She was always so careful with her words.

"Kute, this body is just a temporary vehicle for my soul. It is not who I am. When it takes its last breath, I will still be. Like an article of clothing I no longer need, I will shed this form and yet still be me."

She paused.

"We get so attached sometimes to forms. But I am so much more than my name, and my roles in this lifetime. What will continue after my death? My soul and my love. No one can ever erase that, Kute, so I will always be with you. Maybe not in the physical form. But I will be there."

And then she got up and continued her gardening.

I stared up at the darkening sky, the sun on the

horizon and colors exploding across the sky, considering her wisdom.

Those words stayed with me. And gave me great comfort when she died.

As she had promised, her love didn't disappear upon her death. In fact, I sometimes feel it even more tangibly. I honestly feel her presence and her love after her death in ways I couldn't when her soul was attached to the form.

So surrender the form. Know that love is bigger than the form. True love is beyond the boundaries we create for it. We put all these labels on our relationships: marriage, divorce, dating, breakups, friends, enemies, coworkers, mother, son, father, daughter, neighbor, boss. And they distract from what we are truly called to do. Which is to love. Fully.

The loving is really all that matters. Not the form. Not our personalities. Not the duration. Not how it looks on the surface.

We've got to go deeper.

To the level of the soul.

Let me return to the story of my parents.

As I've mentioned, my parents came from two different worlds. My father is as African as you can get. My mother is as Japanese as you can get. They didn't speak the same language. They didn't eat the same food. And yet they were as committed to each other as any two people could be committed. They knew that their souls had a purpose in this life.

It wasn't like my mother didn't get frustrated with my father. She did. In fact she would often come to me with her troubles. There were moments when I would say, "Why don't you leave?"

But she was unwavering in her commitment to my father and what her soul was here to learn from him. She would say, "He is my soul mate, my divinely appointed partner. It is my mission and purpose to live this life with him."

Theirs was not the love of fairy tales, of being swept off their feet. Of feeling like they fit perfectly together. I've never met two more different people. I'm not sure that they had anything similar on the surface! But when it came to the soul, they had a devotion to the divine that was parallel. My mother was as dedicated as my father. Their souls had an understanding of what they were here to do.

They came together not simply for personal reasons—*meet my needs*—but to serve a bigger purpose: the evolution of their souls in this lifetime. That purpose is what kept them together and moved them through their personal, petty differences.

Love isn't having peace all the time. Love doesn't mean you never argue. Love doesn't mean there aren't conflicts or challenges.

Don't think love means nonconfrontation. Don't think love means not standing up. Don't think love means being a doormat.

Love is fierce.

Love is truth.

And you can't truly love if you aren't being truthful.

When we've been sold the lie that once you find love you'll be in a perfect utopia, and then it starts to get messy, we think something is wrong.

But it isn't.

You've finally entered the arena. Where all the transformation takes place.

At the end of her life, I took my mother to be with my father in Ghana. I felt that the best thing was for them to be together in her final days, to complete their forty-year journey, together. It had been almost nine months since they had seen each other. And when I saw them reunited, the level of love they had for each other astonished me. I'm not talking about romantic love. I'm talking about soul love. It was very humbling for me. Because the love wasn't based on anything from the past. *You didn't do this for me. You disappointed me. You weren't what I thought I wanted.* No. They just loved each other's souls and no matter all that they had been through, their love hadn't wavered. I understood, in those last months, what true love is.

True, unconditional love, is love for the soul.

And he loved her soul and she loved his soul.

And that is what kept them together.

This is what it means to be successful in love. It isn't about how long your relationship lasts, whether it is easy. Whether you get married. But whether you loved fully and surrendered to the purpose you had for each other. Whether you are life partners or not.

When you really understand the purpose of relationships, and can unhook from attachment to the outcome, you are no longer worried about *Are they the one?* They are the one that is in front of you right now. This frees you up to just love. Rather than being in the mind wondering, *Should I love, should I not love?*

Show up. Surrender to the lesson. Love fully.

Don't hold back. Then you are free.

But you don't have to wait for a relationship to do this. Every moment is your invitation to love.

BLOOM

I had a client, Sarah, who had been searching for her soul mate for years. When we first began working together, this aspect of her life was causing her a lot of pain. She came to me, asking: *Where do I find a really great man? I've been going to all these events about manifesting your soul mate, and he still isn't here.*

But here was the problem. When you are fixated on *finding* the one, you aren't *being* the one. You are waiting. Reserving your love for some idealized person in your future. This will never get you what you want.

In our very first session, I had a radical suggestion for Sarah: "Okay, if you want to find your soul mate, you have to be willing to do one thing. Do you think you can do this one thing?"

She nodded eagerly.

I took a deep breath and said: "Stop searching. The energy of searching will not bring the love you seek. In fact, it will repel the very thing you are so eager to attract."

She frowned. This wasn't what she wanted to hear.

I continued, "Right now you are waiting for your life to begin. You are waiting for him to show up before you can love. But trust me, your soul mate doesn't want someone who is holding back their love. If you just live your life today, loving fully and living authentically, you won't have to seek a man. You won't need all the apps you are swiping on. "

She looked at me, confused. "But, Kute, I'm not going to find someone unless I put myself out there."

I smiled. "Sarah, do you not trust the universe? I love your desire to make things happen, but consider that your chasing might be part of the problem. There is a difference between putting yourself out there and pushing yourself out there. Right now, every date you go on, you walk in wondering: *Is this it? Is he the one?* It is possible that men feel your energy as desperation. And then they are turned off, even without knowing why. So, what would happen if you were to let go and surrender the seeking? I know this is going to sound strange and counterintuitive, but surrender to the fact that maybe you'll never meet "the one." You might not get married. Make peace with that. Realize that you can be fulfilled on your own. I'm not saying that it will never happen, but if you can't accept that, you are stuck in fear, and that fear will transmit desperation, and you will be clinging and attached."

She was quiet. She hadn't realized that her endeavors were creating the very situation that she was trying to avoid.

"Trust me. It is time to surrender. Let go of *what if it doesn't happen?* Letting go isn't giving up. Letting go just creates space. Letting go is trusting the universe. Things tend to come to those who don't need them. Love tends to come when you stop chasing it. As you live fully, as you love fully in this moment, the kind of man you want will see you radiating love and he is going to be drawn to you."

This is the path of surrender.

Oprah Winfrey tells the story of getting a part in *The Color Purple*, something she wanted more than she had wanted anything in her life. She had become convinced that she was meant to have this role, despite the fact that she had never acted a day in her life. Two months had passed since her audition, with no word. She finally called the casting director up and he told her, "You have no idea the caliber actors that we have auditioning for this role right now." And as she heard him read off a list of names, she realized: She wasn't going to get the part. This thing that she had been fixated on for months was not going to happen.

As she hung up the phone she realized that she had to let it go. Not in defeat, but in recognition that something better must be coming her way.

She prayed to God: "God, I surrender it all. What would you have me to do now?"

The instant she surrendered, the very moment she finished praying that prayer, she got a phone call. From Steven Spielberg. Offering her the part.

When we grasp and cling and fight for certain outcomes, we aren't open and available.

When we hold back love, waiting, we hold back who we are. When we reserve it for the few, when we think love is something to bestow only to "the one," we shut off that natural flow from our hearts.

Consider the beauty of a flower. The rose isn't just beautiful because we happen to be in the room. When we walk out of the room, it doesn't shrivel up. If you peek back through the doorway, that rose is still emitting its beauty. It is beautiful whether you are there or not. It doesn't shut off its beauty if it thinks you're unworthy. *Oh, you are a murderer or a thief, you don't deserve my beauty*. No. A rose smells as sweet no matter who you are and what you've done, whether you deserve it or not. It isn't waiting for appreciation, or validation. It is just being its nature. Be like a flower.

Our nature is to love. We have just gotten conditioned out of it. **The purpose of life is to return to the love that we are.** To share it, each and every day, with no need for it to be returned, no need for others to be a certain way before we give it to them.

Love, because that is what you have committed to do. Regardless of what another does or doesn't do.

This is to love unconditionally. When you do this, you are free. They may give to you, or they may not give to you. But when you love, you are telegraphing to the universe your readiness. For more love.

This is love at the level of the soul. This is how we were born to love.

When we love this way, it changes every interaction we have.

AN UNLIKELY LOVE STORY

After my first personal trip to India, I was heading to the airport to go home feeling pretty good about all I had learned. I was feeling a little full of myself. Like, I was so spiritual now. I'd shed the ego. Understood my purpose. Nothing could rattle me, now.

I was snaking my way through the immigration line, feeling at peace. As I finally presented my passport to the guard, he was about to slam his stamp down, when he paused.

He looked up at me, and then down at my passport.

Then he closed my passport and said: "Wait here."

Uh oh.

He walked over to some other agents, and they were looking at me suspiciously while he pointed at my pass- port. After a few minutes, I walked over to ask what was going on.

"Be quiet!" they said forcefully.

I backed away. I was getting a little afraid now.

I stood waiting, quietly, as instructed. After a few more minutes, the agent walked over to me and said, "We think your passport is a fake." He showed me where my signature was a little smudged and then pulled me out of the line to sit next to an armed guard.

Okay, now I wasn't a little afraid, I was really afraid. I was having visions of an Indian prison. Fears that I'd be locked away and no one would know where to find me.

I didn't know what to do.

The worst-case scenarios were going through my head. I began to panic and my mind started to spiral out of control.

Eventually I tried to get a grip on myself. I had just spent all of these months in India. It can't have been for nothing. It was time to remember what I'd learned on my journey.

I closed my eyes and reflected on the great ones. *In this moment, what would Jesus do? What would Gandhi do? What would the great ones do?*

Well, I knew first they would accept and surrender to the situation exactly as it was. Okay, no more resistance.

And then I closed my eyes and tried to feel for what would be the appropriate action.

And what I felt deep in my heart was that great ones would simply send love.

Now, love is not always the first thing you think about with an armed guard standing over your shoulder. At first, I resisted. *I don't want to send love. I'm mad. My passport is not fake. They are mistaken. And because of them, I'm going to miss my flight! This is wrong.*

But I felt the call of the great ones. If the purpose of

life is to love, it is easy to love when you feel like it, but it is more potent to love when you don't. That's where the growth is. And that's when it counts.

That is greatness.

Don't demand others change first. Don't wait. You, at your core, are love. Share it. Be it. Live it. Be like a flower, right now, and radiate.

I closed my eyes and I started sending these guards, and every worker in the airport, love. Simple love. Pure love.

This didn't mean that I went over and hugged them. But I sent them love from my heart.

When you choose to love, sure, it can be a blessing for the other person, but it is more a blessing for you. I felt my attitude shift. I realized that they were just human, trying to earn a paycheck, trying to keep their country safe. It wasn't about me. I didn't need to take it so personally.

It felt a bit odd, to be sitting there loving in the midst of the crowded airport. But I knew, deep down, it was what I was called to do. And I felt a peace.

I kid you not. Within five minutes of me deciding to send love, the original guard walked over, handed me back my passport, and said, "You can leave now."

I didn't even know what to say. *What do you mean? After all that?*

But I grabbed my passport, thanked the universe, and hurried to my gate. My flight had been delayed (it was India, after all), and I got on board and made it home. None of my fears came true. I experienced no harm. In fact, India had provided one more lesson.

This is the magic of surrender.

Resist and hate and demand change from the other person.

Or surrender and love. And you'll never lose.

There is nothing preventing you from loving every person you encounter. Nothing needs to change in order for you to love. Now.

Your annoying neighbor. Your mother-in-law. Your ex-husband. Your ex-wife. Your toddler. The tired and short-tempered server. The president of your country.

They are all opportunities to love. It's your choice.

This is the call of the great ones. They didn't grant favor to a select few. They knew that the world was their home, and the human race their family.

They decided to love, fully, no matter what. Every day of their lives.

TO BE A NEIGHBOR

I like you just the way you are.

Eight words. They seem simple. But they hold immense power.

They come from Fred Rogers.

Mister Rogers did not hold a position of prestige or power. But he had immense influence. Not over politicians. Not over business leaders.

No. Instead he had influence over children.

He knew how important it was to meet children where they were. He didn't know what their home environment was like. He didn't know what kind of education they received. But he knew what all children needed.

Love. And to understand that who they were mattered. That they were worthy of love, no matter what.

His PBS television program, *Mister Rogers' Neighborhood*, was an un-showy, slow-paced program that tackled different situations that were common to all children. Loss. Learning how to deal with frustration. Imagination. Feelings.

When asked what he was trying to create through it, Fred Rogers said: "an atmosphere that allows people to be comfortable enough to be who they are."[1]

This is the heart of love, isn't it? We can't love others until we love ourselves. Until we know that within us is everything we need. That there is no shortage of love to go around.

Mister Rogers knew how important it was to remind people that they were worthy. That there was nothing they needed to change about themselves to be deserving of love. It is something that we forget. He wanted children to remember. He wanted us all to remember.

Despite the fame he acquired throughout his life, and the many people who asked him for interviews, he was never good at answering questions. He always seemed to turn the questions back around to whomever he was with. He loved getting to know people, and was deeply interested in them.

His favorite quote was from *The Little Prince*: "What is essential is invisible to the eyes." It hung from the wall in his office. He knew that it was what was within us that mattered.

"It is not the honors and the prizes and the fancy outsides of life which ultimately nourish our souls," he once said in a speech. "It's the knowing that we can be trusted, that we never have to fear the truth, that the bedrock of our very being is good stuff."[2]

He was always trying to discern what made each person who came into his life special. There was no judgment within him, only curiosity. If a child came to him angry, or guarded, or misbehaving, he didn't admonish him or her, but came down to their level and met them where they were. With love. With acceptance. With the desire for understanding.

Mister Rogers was married for fifty years. But he didn't reserve his love for only his wife.

Mister Rogers had two sons of his own. But he didn't give his love only to his children.

He gave of himself, fully, to all who came in contact with him. Each and every day.

This doesn't mean he didn't have boundaries. That he said yes to anything anyone ever asked of him.

No. He knew when he needed to be done for the day. He knew when something was against his integrity and was firm about what he stood for.

But he emitted love; he shared the essence of his being, every day of his life. He bloomed fully, loved fully, each and every day.

And changed the world in the process.

What would it mean for you to get back in touch with the truth of who you are? To know that within you is all the love you've ever tried to seek outside? And to be who you are truly meant to be is to share that love with others?

What would it mean to reframe success in love and realize that love is not something to distract you from life, and protect you from hurt, but to bring you even deeper into who you are meant to be?

You might get married.

You might not get married.

You might get divorced.

You might not get divorced.

You might become a parent.

You might not become a parent.

But none of that has anything to do with the amount of love you can share with the world in each moment.

You are love. You were born to love.

To love without fear.

To love no matter what.

Not because you feel like loving. Not because everything is going well.

To love now.

Right now, can you love? Right now, can you love more?

The answer is always yes.

Love is freedom. And the greatest freedom is to love.

CHAPTER SEVEN

UNLOCKING THE MAGIC

GREATNESS

YESTERDAY IS GONE.

Tomorrow may never come.

This moment is your only guarantee.

Stop looking somewhere else. The magic is right in front of you.

Within you. Around you. Above you. Below you.

There is nowhere to get to.

This is it.

There really are no ordinary moments, if you are truly paying attention.

It's not just about what you accomplish in the major moments of your life.

It's about how you live in the seemingly mundane.

This makes all the difference.

Then every moment becomes precious, every moment, a privilege.

And the magic of each moment can reveal itself to you.

TWO VERSUS TWO HUNDRED

When I was twenty years old, I decided to put on my first seminar.

I spent a month promoting it in anticipation of lots of people showing up. The night of the seminar, I was hoping a hundred people would attend. From a very young age, I had dreams of doing seminars with thousands of people, but I knew I needed to start small.

The day of the event, I got a haircut, put on my best suit and tie. Took some deep breaths. Headed to the hotel whose small conference room I had rented.

It was 7:45 a.m. The event started at eight. I walked into the room.

And there were two people sitting there.

One of them was my friend, who had brought *her* friend.

My heart sank.

I had put all this time and energy into this seminar, and spreading the word. I was heartbroken. Two people? Really?

I walked into the room and approached my friend Barbara.

"Thanks so much for coming," I said as I sat down next to her, trying to ignore all the empty seats around.

She introduced me to her friend.

I shook her hand. And then said: "Look, obviously we didn't get a good turnout. I'm thinking I'll cancel tonight and you can both come back another night, when more people are able to attend."

Barbara looked at me, confused. "What do you mean, 'cancel'?"

"Well," I said with a nervous laugh. "No one is here!"

She looked at her friend and then she looked back at me.

"What do you mean, 'no one is here'? I'm here. My friend is here. We paid for our parking and we want our seminar!"

I looked at her like *you can't be serious.*

But she was serious.

"We are not *no one.* We are two people who have

come to listen and be inspired. We're ready. So get your-self together! Let's go."

To be honest, I was a little mad at her insistence. But because her friend was with her, I had to take a step back. I realized she was right. I was devaluing the two people in front of me because I was attached to having two hun-dred in front of me.

I nodded and said, "Okay. I will be back."

And I went to the restroom and cried. This wasn't what I had wanted. A part of me felt ashamed. Like I was a failure for only having two people in the room. But another part of me knew that this feeling of disappoint-ment was because I was wrapped up in ego, in finding my own worth in how many people attended. Deep down, I knew I wasn't coming from a pure place.

As I stood in that bathroom and stared at myself in the mirror, I had to get real. *Am I in this to truly serve oth-ers? Or to feed my ego? Of course it would be wonderful to have two hundred people in that room. But if I am in this to truly serve, here are two people to serve. So I need to show up and give them everything I've got.*

I dried my tears. Walked back into the near-empty conference room. Ran up onstage, and delivered a two-hour seminar with all of my energy, sincerity, authenticity, and passion.

Those two women cried, laughed, were transformed, and thanked me on their way out.

After they left, I sat in that room, by myself, looking around at the empty chairs. It is a moment I will never forget. Because from that moment on, I made a commitment. No matter how many people show up, I will always give my all. I will never again consider canceling. I will know that even if just one person benefits from my offering, I will have done my part.

A few years later I came to believe this even more strongly.

When I first started making videos and posting them to YouTube, I had no idea, other than the small numbers ticking up in the corner of the screen when I checked my metrics, whether they made any difference in people's lives. One day, I was in Japan and had traveled to this remote village to visit a small temple, when a young woman walked up to me as I entered the courtyard.

She said, in Japanese, "Excuse me, are you Kute Blackson?"

I looked at her in shock. Did I know this woman? "Yes, I am," I said with a cautious smile.

She smiled back. "I watch your videos on YouTube. You made a video about forgiving your parents."

She paused. She was standing next to an older woman, and now she gestured to her. "This is my mother. We weren't speaking for over a year. We'd had a disagreement about a relationship, and weren't seeing eye to eye, and honestly, I was angry at how she reacted and what I took to be her judgment. But because of your video, I was able to see that she meant well, and I chose to forgive my mother. Today, we have a relationship, because of you."

They both smiled and bowed slightly and said: "*Arigato.*" *Thank you.*

I bowed back, and they walked off. I watched the form of these two women, walking together, as tears filled my eyes.

Flashing through my memories were all the times I almost gave up at the beginning of my career and several times along the way. When I was hungry and could barely pay the bills. When I wasn't sure whether I was making a difference. When I had no clients.

I began to make videos. It wasn't always easy. I didn't

always feel like it. I really didn't even know if anyone would watch them.

But at that moment, in the middle of nowhere, I thought: *What if I had given up? What if I hadn't bothered making that video because I thought it wouldn't make a difference?*

It didn't have ten million views. But it didn't matter. It touched this one woman.

And it transformed her relationship with her mother.

Was all the struggle worth it?

Absolutely.

We think to be great we have to always do big things. But we don't.

We just have to start where we are, and do what we feel called in our heart to do to make a difference, in each moment of every day.

This is the path of greatness.

IT'S ALL IN THE DETAILS

Jiro Ono knows that it is the small steps that lead to significant impact.

He is a ninety-three-year-old sushi chef. His simple,

ten-seat restaurant in a subway station in Tokyo is one of only one hundred restaurants to receive the coveted three stars from the Michelin guide. He serves nothing but sushi. No rolls. No drinks. No appetizers. Simple *nigiri*. A slice of fish over rice. Yet they take reservations months in advance.

He is notoriously exacting. In the freshness of the fish. The sharpness of the knives. The temperature of the rice. The placement on the plate.

Even though he is one of the best, he is always striving to be better.

"I do the same thing over and over. Improving bit by bit. There is always a yearning to achieve more."[1]

There is no detail that is too small for his meticulous attention.

Without the small details, it would not add up to the most delicious sushi of your life.

It is in the small that the seeds of greatness take root.

I always wanted to do great things with my life. And for a time, I thought if it wasn't big enough, it wasn't worth doing. I questioned the efforts I made, wondering if they made any difference.

Sometimes we think that to be great is to do big things.

To make a difference means you must invent something. Build a company. Run for office.

But revolutions don't always begin with grand plans. Change is enacted when someone dares to acknowledge a problem, looks around, and sees that no one else is doing anything about it.

And then does their small part.

It always starts small.

Greta Thunberg says she never set out to be an activist. She never wanted to be in front of cameras. She didn't desire a platform, a cause, or to upend her childhood.

But she could no longer stomach the blatant disregard for truth.

She was a fifteen-year-old kid. Didn't expect that she would make much of a difference. But she had to do something.

And that one small choice spiraled into a global movement.

Don't misunderstand me. I know you want to do great things with your life. It is what you were born to do. But greatness isn't always extravagant.

Jesus wasn't born in some fancy palace but in a little manger in the stable.

Buddha wasn't enlightened in the palace he was born in, but under a simple bodhi tree.

The seeds of greatness are in the small moments of your life. The hundreds of different choices we make throughout our lifetime.

Greatness is not lived on the mountaintop but in the mess of everyday life.

People say, *Don't sweat the small stuff.*

I say greatness is in the small stuff.

AN ODE TO MY MOTHER

I admit that I am someone who has chased the extraordinary.

I am someone who has been focused on making the most of life, I wanted to see it all. I've gone to Machu Picchu, I've visited the pyramids of Egypt, seen the towering skyline of Singapore, marveled at the Taj Mahal, and swum in the beautiful blue ocean in Bali. I've traveled to over fifty countries and had some of the most unimaginable experiences. And while I recognize the power that travel holds to break you out of your routine, that it can melt the layers and reveal parts of yourself that you'd lost access to, there are times when I feel like I may have missed something.

I left home when I was eighteen years old and never looked back. Sure, I came back to visit now and again, but I realize, looking back now, that because I was so focused on building my career and traveling the world, and doing and accomplishing and becoming, that I took my relationship with my mother for granted. I figured I would have plenty of time to spend with her, once I was done building my career and had achieved all my goals.

Obviously, I regretted this choice as soon as I learned she had cancer. But I couldn't get that time back.

I remember a phone call I had with Amir around this time, my friend whom I met on the train platform in India. I was going to be back in India and wanted to meet up with him. So I called him and was talking about all the plans I had and meetings I had scheduled and when I could squeeze in a visit with him in between meetings.

I heard silence on the other end of the phone.

And in his quiet, wise way, he said, "Kute, you are such a busy man, constantly making all these plans. But remember, real life is what happens in the in-between. Don't be running so fast that you miss it."

He was so right.

When I visited my mother when she was sick, I vowed not to take any of it for granted. For the first time since I was eighteen, I lived with her, sometimes for a week at a time. Saw her in the morning over tea. Drove her to doctor's appointments. Cut up the cucumbers with her as we made sushi. Took walks in the park.

My eyes were opened and I saw who she truly was, as if for the very first time. I had always thought my father was the great one because he was the powerhouse, the famous one, the miracle worker.

I was wrong.

I didn't understand how small acts of everyday kindness and love can add up to a life that is truly great.

How she cooked me dinner every night with so much love.

How she recognized my love for soccer and made me my own soccer kit.

How she sacrificed her own clothes and needs to be able to send me to judo class after school.

How her insistence that I study Japanese for an hour a day, five days a week, despite how much I complained, was a great gift. I'm able to speak it fluently today. Because of her.

People often tell me how great they think I am. The truth is, I would not be who I am today, without her love.

I would not be doing what I'm doing, serving the way I'm serving, loving the way I'm able to love, without her support.

The ego loves to consider how great it is. But we are never great on our own.

We become great on the backs of those who have loved us into being, through small, simple, everyday acts.

Mister Rogers knew this. When he walked up onstage to receive the Emmy Lifetime Achievement Award in 1997, he did not give a long speech. He said simply this: "So many people have helped me to come to this night. Some of you are here, some are far away, some are even in heaven. All of us have special ones who have loved us into being. Would you just take, along with me, ten seconds to think of the people who have helped you become who you are? Those who have cared about you and wanted what was best for you in life. Ten seconds of silence. I'll watch the time."[2]

He then looked at his watch as he let silence envelop the room.

People at first shifted uncomfortably in their seats. Silence isn't something we're accustomed to. But then the cameras began to capture these actors thinking of the people who had loved them. Tears began to brim in their well-made-up eyes, lips began to quiver as people reflected on who helped bring them into being, who allowed them to end up at this glamorous, star-studded night.

After the promised ten seconds, Mister Rogers looked up and said: "Whomever you've been thinking about, how pleased they must be to know the difference you think they've made."

And then he walked off the stage.

We've long worshiped a certain set of heroes. Marvel characters, athletes, actors, and supermodels.

I think today we are finally beginning to understand who the true heroes are.

Schoolteachers. Doctors. Nursing home aides. Grocery store clerks. Delivery workers. Sanitation workers.

No one would dare argue today that being a grocery store employee isn't important work. They keep us fed.

No one can say that nursing isn't a noble profession. They literally keep us alive.

No one can say that to care for the elderly isn't a sacred call.

We finally realize that the great ones aren't the ones

necessarily being covered by the media. They aren't always those with millions of followers online or on the front cover of *Time* magazine. They were the ones behind the scenes.

I'm not saying that we all need to change our jobs.

But we must reframe what it means to be great. **We must realize that it isn't the big moments that make us great, but who we are in each moment of our lives.**

It isn't about what you do. It is about who you are being. In your job. In your marriage. In your parenting. Around your community.

It is giving your all to the ordinary moments of life.

And then we realize that there are no ordinary moments.

THE SPIRITUAL SHIFT

Rob was one of my clients who was incredibly successful and loved his job. He worked in the financial industry and made a lot of money for himself and his clients. As we worked together, he began to question whether he was on the right path. He wondered if he should be doing something different with his life. He wanted to be of more service.

He began to brainstorm different ways he could have a greater impact on the world. Maybe he could become a musician and tour the country inspiring people. Maybe he could train to become a life coach. Because he felt like his current job just wasn't making a difference in the world.

But I wanted Rob to see that nothing needed to change in his life in order for him to do great things.

"Rob, let me ask you a question. Is there anyone who can sing better than you?"

"Yes. Of course," he said, with humility.

"Is there someone who can play guitar better than you?"

"Definitely."

"Is there anyone else who can make money like you do?"

He considered, and then shook his head. "No. I'm one of the best."

I laughed, amused that he recognized his gift so clearly. "Well, then, let me ask you. Do you know what it takes to feed starving children? Money. Do you know what it takes to build schools in areas that do not have access to education? Money. So do you know what it takes to serve humanity?"

He looked at me with a smile. "Money."

"Exactly," I said. "No matter how hard you pray, your prayers won't feed the world, will they?"

He shook his head.

"People think that to be spiritual you must give up money. But true spirituality isn't meditating in the clouds, it is doing your part right now, with what you've got. So consider that your job, which provides you with so much money, can actually be a vehicle for the work you want to do."

Rob's eyes lit up. He loved his job. He was good at it. It brought him joy. The only problem was that he thought it wasn't spiritual enough to be of service.

So I turned to him and said, matter-of-factly, "I admire your intention to try to lead a more spiritual life. But just know that, really, there is nothing that is not spiritual. There is nothing that is not spirit. The ego thinks it is separate, so it fools you into thinking that you need to seek spirituality, because it thinks spirituality is separate from itself. That spirituality is something you have to *do*. **But when you realize that what you are is spirit, then you see that you can't not be spiritual even if you tried.** It is a state of being. It is what you are. It's not about what you do or don't do."

I paused.

"So whether you decided to be a stockbroker, or a musician or a waitress or a taxi driver, the form is less important. Spirituality is what you are and that awareness that you bring into what you do. So if you know *why* you are making money, every day you go to your office and you know exactly what you are working for. It is no longer just about shareholders or pleasing the CEO, but about doing your best, and knowing that whatever you earn is not just for yourself and your gratification, to enhance your money, status, influence, and power, but can be utilized to do great things for the world and to serve all of humanity."

When Rob left my office, there was a spring to his step that I hadn't seen recently: because he had surrendered the idea that he needed to do something different to be great. He realized that right now was the very moment he'd been waiting for. He could begin to live his greatness every day, no matter what he chose to do.

It didn't require that he sell everything and move to the Himalayas. It didn't require him to shave his head and change his name. It didn't require him to alter his diet and subscribe to some exotic religion.

It just required that he see everything as sacred and hold every moment with reverence.

TO FALL IN LOVE WITH LIFE

I cannot tell you what I would give to spend one more day with my mother.

I would honestly sell everything I had for the chance to be with her one more time.

And yet on that day, do you know what I'd do?

I wouldn't want to travel with her to some special place or go eat at a fancy restaurant.

No. I'd just want to sit across from her at the kitchen table, with a cup of tea, and hours to cook a meal together. Talk. Laugh. Reminisce. The simple things.

What I wouldn't give for that. It would be priceless.

And yet I had thousands of days with her!

But I didn't see how special it was. I was blind to it.

Today, I call that a *sacred regret*. It is sacred because it propelled me to not make that mistake again.

As I've said, her death compelled me to mend my relationship with my father. I visit him in Ghana every three months. Ghana is not an easy place to get to from

L.A. It takes me two full days to get there, but I do it, and spend a few days with him. People ask me what we do. Ghana is an incredible country with a rich cultural life, but I tell people: I do nothing. I sit with my father. I watch him eat. I watch him sleep. Sometimes we talk, but often, we say nothing.

But in the nothing is everything.

I think we've had our own wake-up call this year in how amazing our ordinary existence truly is. In 2020, with the world in lockdown, we began to appreciate our "normal" lives in a totally different way. The ordinary began to feel extraordinary. Even though before the lockdown, we maybe weren't happy with our job or the details of our lives, in quarantine, we would do anything to get back to it. To be able to get a haircut. Give your neighbor a hug. Attend a meeting with your coworkers. Get on a plane and go somewhere. Send your kid to school.

We recognize now that these are small miracles.

So how did we get to the point when we just took it all for granted?

How did we get so jaded that we looked at our lives and said: *Is this all?*

I want you to learn what it means to experience the

magic of surrender. Not just as you face the big moments of life.

But in the small moments as well. The everyday moments. Where life is truly lived.

When you are running errands, sitting with your parents, taking out the trash, washing the car, making love, taking your dog for a walk, playing with your kids.

Each of these moments is spiritual when you are fully present for them.

It's time to slow down. Savor life fully.

And realize this moment is the most important moment of your life.

We think these moments are unimportant. Things to get through on our way to something bigger.

But to miss the miracle of this moment is to miss the miracle that is your life.

And to miss the many ways that you can make a difference. Right now.

THE RIPPLE EFFECT

When I was about eight years old, I met Mr. Johnson.

He was my gym teacher.

He was very strict. The kids at school were always a little scared of him.

But honestly, Mr. Johnson is someone who truly changed my life.

I would not be who I am today without his influence.

He was my teacher for about eight years, as well as my soccer coach. One day, when I was a teenager, we were out on the soccer field playing a practice match.

Our team was losing. About halfway through the game, Mr. Johnson said he needed to go get something and headed back into the school building.

He was gone for about a half hour. Well, being kids, we started messing around, being silly, throwing the football instead of kicking it. Our team was losing anyway. It didn't really matter and we didn't care.

And then Mr. Johnson walked back onto the field, furious.

"Everyone, in my office, now!" he shouted.

We trudged back in the building and into his small office. He didn't say a word. Just turned on a video of one of the best soccer teams of all time, Liverpool F.C., and made us watch them play for the next hour and a half.

Finally, he stopped the tape and turned toward us, his eyes still burning with disappointment.

"I want you to know that the way you all were behaving out there was a disgrace and unacceptable."

We shifted uncomfortably in our seats.

"I don't care what the score is. I don't care whether you win or lose. I care whether you show up and give your best."

He paused and looked at each one of us. We hung our heads in shame. We knew he was right.

"You thought I wasn't watching. I was watching from the window the entire time. But you've got to know that it doesn't matter who is watching. You have to always show up. You give it one hundred percent. Not because I'm watching, or somebody else is watching, but because it is the right thing to do. Then you can have pride in yourself. You don't do it for your team, or your teacher, or the fans. But so that you can look yourself in the mirror at the end of each day and feel a peace when you go to sleep at night."

He paused.

"It is better to lose giving everything than to win holding back."

He went on to talk about the team on the screen, how they became the best team in the world by giving their all. That greatness wasn't about the scoreboard, necessarily, but was a choice about who you were being in each moment.

He then turned around and walked out the door.

That was a life-changing moment for me. And for our team.

He planted in me the desire to be truly great.

I wasn't the best soccer player. We weren't the best team. But after that talk, we began to win. We began to defeat teams that were much more talented than us on paper. Because we were playing full out, with our whole hearts, with every ounce of effort we had to give.

We get so caught up in comparing ourselves to others that sometimes we don't even start. Because we're never going to be as good. We're never going to have the same impact. We'll never garner as many followers or change as many lives. So why even try?

The only thing that is required is to do our best. In each and every moment.

Now, Mr. Johnson probably doesn't remember me today. But he changed my life. And through changing my life, he has gone on to impact millions.

Millions? Really, Kute? Yes, really. Think about it. He has had an impact on every person that I have an impact on. I would not serve the way I do without his influence.

And if he changed my life, I'm sure he changed other students' lives. And those students go on to impact others through their own dedication. And on and on.

Now, Mr. Johnson was just a gym teacher in South London in the 1980s.

But he wasn't just a gym teacher.

He was one of the great ones.

He may not have known the scope of his impact.

But we don't have to know. Obviously, it is nice to learn how we've inspired others. It feels good to know we've made a difference.

But we don't have to be recognized.

Greatness doesn't require a special title.

You may never know the impact that you have. But that doesn't mean you shouldn't give fully to each moment of your life.

Maybe you're not the one performing the slam-dunk. But you pass the ball to Michael Jordan. You are equally a part of what goes up on that scoreboard.

Maybe you aren't Greta Thunberg, but the person who first told her about the climate crisis and lit the fire in her heart. You are a part of her trajectory.

So when I hear a mother say, "I'm just a mother." No. You are creating an entire life. When I hear a teacher say,

"I'm just a teacher." No. You are the foundation that allows the next generation to grow.

Those who do great things are not great in a vacuum. They were loved into being. By people like you.

Which makes you just as great as they are.

It doesn't matter if people know your name or if you win any awards.

You don't even have to be extraordinarily talented. I have always been pretty average. But I always show up fully, with the commitment to give everything. That is what helps me access the extraordinary potential that is inside each and every one of us.

Give your all to each moment, and that is when the magic happens.

Then the ordinary transforms. The ordinary becomes extraordinary through your intention. You realize there are no ordinary moments, because how you meet each moment is what makes it what it is.

THE POWER OF A MOSQUITO

The world needs nothing more than for you to be open to what this very moment is calling for.

Many years ago, I traveled to Bihar, the poorest state

in India. One of my dearest friends wanted me to meet someone who had educated over a hundred thousand children in this state, where the literacy rate is just 18 percent.

His name was Dhirendra Sharma.

I arrived at one of his educational centers, very excited to meet him, thinking he was going to be some important, big-shot guy. And as I stood, waiting, two guys walked up to me. They were young, no older than me. So I figured they were here to take me to meet Dhirendra Sharma.

One of them reached out and shook my hand. "Hi, I'm Dhirendra." And I realized that right in front of me was Sharma himself.

He could probably see the shock on my face. But I didn't understand how such a young guy could have already accomplished so much.

He began to give me a tour around his center.

And I learned a bit of his story.

He had moved to the city when he was nineteen and started to learn English from the tourists. Then he began to teach what he'd learned to the children he came in contact with. First it was one-on-one. Then word of his teaching spread, and soon he was teaching five children, ten children, twenty children at a time. Eventually, word spread throughout the state and thousands started to come to him.

Today he has over forty centers throughout the region that provide education as well as vocational skills for tens of thousands of kids, including how to craft a résumé and tips on succeeding in job interviews.

Today, he wanted me to speak to some of these teenagers. I wasn't sure what I had to share, but told them a bit of my story and then stayed to answer their questions. They were wide-eyed, curious, thrilled with the opportunity to be able to converse with me in English. In them, I could see the future of India and felt so inspired.

Afterward, they swarmed around me to tell me their own stories and ask me questions. Most came from extreme poverty, but were eager to share their big dreams now that they could read and write, and speak English.

When I sat down with Sharma afterward, I was a bit in awe of all he had accomplished by such a young age and told him as much.

He looked at me with a smile. "Kute, I'm not anything great. I'm not a visionary. I'm a practical idealist. I'm just interested in doing what I can with what I have, in this moment. There is nothing great about responding to a need. It is simply human, to see a need and respond."

As he accompanied me to the front door, I asked him about the most fulfilling part of what he does.

He paused, considering. And then he said:

"Kute, these children, when I first meet them, they don't look me in the eye. They think they have nothing to offer. They have low self-esteem. They have been brought up begging. Some don't have parents. But today, after learning to speak English, and learning to read, they look me in the eyes. They have pride in what they are doing, how they are learning, how they are changing their lives and the lives of their families. That is my reward. The light in their eyes. The knowledge of all they have to give the world."

I shook his hand and then turned to go. My mind was churning, thinking about how I could make a big impact. But as I turned to walk away, he said something that really struck me: "Kute, don't get caught up in trying to do some big thing. Don't think that any action is too small."

He smiled.

"If you think small things can't make a difference,

remember the mosquito!" he said. "They can keep you up all night, an annoying buzzing in your ear. They are the deadliest animals on this planet. Small can be mighty. Never forget that."

I smiled and waved. Those words have stayed with me.

To surrender doesn't have to be a massive undertaking, but can start with a simple step.

In fact, greatness has never been something that you are granted, but a seed you are born with. It is something that you nurture, something you develop, choice by choice, and moment by moment.

Don't think any choice is too small. Because if I think it is too small, and you think it is too small, and seven billion people decide it is too small, then no one does anything.

Each person on earth, doing their part, making bold choices, every moment of their lives, is what truly changes the world.

It doesn't have to be about the environment. It doesn't have to be about injustice. It can be as simple as sending a text message to someone who is lonely. It could be as small as writing a thank-you note. Making the phone call to have an honest conversation. Checking in with a neighbor. Eating a bit less meat. Using less single-use plastic. Donating a few dollars to a cause you care about. Sitting down and letting your spouse know what you appreciate about them. Mentoring someone who is just beginning in your industry.

Each of these actions has an impact.

You alter the world by adding your voice.

I'm not saying your voice is going to be the single factor that changes everything. But it will be a contribution to the symphony of humanity.

So surrender to now. Surrender to the moment.

This moment is it. There is no future greatness.

There is only greatness in the choices you make today.

LEADING THE WAY

There was once a woman who, despite being born into a situation where she had no say in her own life, no control over where she lived, or how she filled her days, decided to take power into her own hands.

She was a slave. The lowest of the low.

And yet today everyone knows her name.

She was a woman who was not content to be bound

by chains for the rest of her days. So rather than succumb to the pain of her given lot in life, she surrendered instead to the call inside her heart.

The call of freedom.

She decided to become a master of her destiny rather than a prisoner of her fate.

Despite the risk of death, she escaped to Philadelphia and, more important, the freedom of the North.

She had done what many deemed impossible. And yet once there, she realized she didn't want to keep this gift to herself. She thought of her sister and her sister's children, still enslaved, her precious niece almost at the age where she could be auctioned off.

She decided to jeopardize her own freedom, to save her family.

Thus Harriet Tubman set off on an endeavor that would come to define her life: risking her own life to grant her people the freedom she knew they deserved.

This, my friends, is what surrender looks like.

Now, to become the most influential figure in the movement of the Underground Railroad is no small feat. But Tubman did not set out to become the greatest. She set out to make a difference in one life. To save her sister. And once that was accomplished, she came back for her brother. She then listened to her soul and realized that this was her calling, and she surrendered to it. And she became the Harriet Tubman we know of today.

There were risks. I'm sure she was scared. To put her own life on the line over and over, terror stalking her at every step, around every corner, is bravery beyond words. But she had fully surrendered to the cause. She knew she might die. That it was dangerous. She knew those in her care might die. But it was worth it.

Freedom was worth it.

She could have saved just herself. She had made it to safety. But she surrendered to the call. She was following her guidance. This was a mission bigger than herself.

She did not know how many people she would save. Every trip could have been her last. She was not concerned with her legacy, but with the people who needed her. She couldn't keep score, she had to stay focused on the North Star, which led the way to freedom, and the song in her heart that reminded her that freedom was worth risking everything.

Her courage, her determination, her commitment is what made her great.

Her efforts did not stop at the Underground Railroad.

She went on to be the first woman to lead an armed military raid during the Civil War.

She built a nursing home for African Americans on her property in Auburn, New York, after the war.

She was helping people, every single day of her life.

She was always looking for the need, and seeing how she could fill it.

She did not have elaborate plans for greatness.

But she knew that she was made for freedom, and she was committed to helping everyone achieve that goal.

To surrender is not being fixated on the big things to change the world, but on the small things you can do to be of service.

To surrender is not to always win the game, but in playing with your whole heart.

Surrender is not about what you do. But who you are being. In every moment of your life.

So whenever you think you aren't enough, busy comparing yourself to others.

Whenever you're wondering about whether you make a difference, or questioning your existence.

I want you to remember that you are already great.

You. Are. Already. Great.

The fact that you are alive is proof of that greatness.

Greatness is what is breathing you.

Greatness is what is beating your heart.

Greatness is your birthright.

Surrender to your greatness.

A tree doesn't question its gifts, it just grows. It spreads its branches and produces leaves so we can enjoy the shade beneath it.

It knows what it is here to do. It does its job fully.

Every day it becomes a little bit more of what it was meant to be. Even though at the beginning it is a small acorn.

In fifty years, it towers fifty feet.

It is the nature of the sun to shine. It is the nature of the moon to glow. It is the nature of the rivers to flow.

It is your nature to awaken your greatness.

Regardless of your past, it is never too late. You are not a prisoner of your fate.

When you surrender, you create a new soul's destiny.

To surrender doesn't have to be rocket science. It does not require a PhD.

All you need is the willingness to show up, be open, and allow life to lead you.

I promise you, it will.

Maybe not to where you expect. But somewhere even better.

Surrender changes everything.

It gives you access to more joy. More love. More power. More fulfillment. More freedom. More impact. More grace. More aliveness.

Surrender is the password to freedom.

Letting go leads to more. A life beyond anything you could plan for yourself.

To live this way will change your life.

And in turn, will change the world.

This is what you were born for.

This is why you are here.

No more waiting. No more excuses.

The universe is calling you now.

Will you say yes?

ACKNOWLEDGMENTS

I owe a deep gratitude to each person who has ever touched my life. Whether we shared a brief moment or a long-lasting connection, you have all contributed to the fabric of who I am today, which allowed for the birth of this book. Thank you.

However, I do wish to thank some specific people who have not only helped to bring this book to the world but have been there for me throughout the process.

First, deepest gratitude to my editor, Sara Carder. You believed in me, as well as the message of this book, from the very first time we met. Thank you for your enthusiasm, trust, and passion for this book, and your recognition of the importance of its message.

Also a big thank-you to the amazing team at TarcherPerigee/Penguin Random House: Rachel Ayotte, Jess Morphew, Lorie Pagnozzi, Farin Schlussel, Alex Casement, Victoria Adamo, Megan Newman, and Lindsay Gordon.

To Cindy DiTiberio, you were the best partner I could have asked for. You helped me birth the soul of this book with your brilliant brainstorming and amazing writing/editing talents. You went above and beyond. Thank you for your relentless dedication to making the book amazing. It has been a privilege to collaborate with you.

To my agent, Roger Freet. I appreciate your belief in me and my message, as well as your expert shepherding of this book. I look forward to many more.

To my dedicated team at The Blackson Group. Cesar Franco, your unwavering commitment to spreading the message and transforming lives inspires me. It's been an honor to have you on my team for so many years. To Heather Godfrey, your devotion to the work and willingness to do whatever it takes is the backbone of our success and makes a difference in so many lives. Thank you for your love and loyalty. To Belen Vidal, thank you for showing up daily with grace, authenticity, kindness, and for being a blessing.

To my dear friends, thank you for being there through it all. Gina Cloud, your friendship and love has been a true gift over the years. Jeannie Kang, thanks for being a big sister and always looking out for me. Matthew and Deborah Mitchell, thank you for showing me constant unconditional love.

Last, to my father. You are a great man, and it is a privilege to be your son in this lifetime. Much of who I am today is because of you. Through your example you showed me the real meaning of surrender, love, service, and faith. I love you.

NOTES

Chapter 1. How to Get Out of Your Own Way

1. Nelson Mandela, *The Long Walk to Freedom* (Boston: Little, Brown, 1995), 95.
2. Angus Gibson and Jo Menell, dirs., *Mandela: Son of Africa, Father of a Nation*, 1996; South Africa and the United States, Palm Pictures documentary.

Chapter 2. Level Up

1. Ray Dalio, *Principles: Life and Work* (New York: Simon & Schuster, 2017), 135.
2. Ibid., 137.
3. *The Howard Stern Show*, interview with Trevor Noah, November 4, 2019.
4. Bryan Stevenson, *Just Mercy: A Story of Justice and Redemption* (New York: Spiegel & Grau, 2014).
5. *Oprah's SuperSoul Conversations*, episode 101, "Bryan Stevenson: The Power of Mercy and Forgiveness," January 4, 2019.

Chapter 3. The Ultimate Improvisation

1. *Oprah's SuperSoul Conversations*, "Lady Gaga: Heal Through Kindness," November 6, 2019, 61:17, https://podtail.com/en/podcast/oprah-s-supersoul-conversations/lady-gaga-heal-through-kindness/.

2. Ibid.

3. "Bruce Lee Be as Water My Friend," YouTube, Terry Lee McBride, August 14, 2013. https://www.youtube.com/watch?v=cJMwBwFj5nQ

4. Letter from John Steinbeck, to his son Thom, November 10, 1958, https://www.penguin.co.uk/articles/2015/read-john-steinbeck-s-letter-of-fatherly-advice-to-his-son.html.

5. *Inside the Actors Studio*, "Dave Chappelle," season 12, episode 11, aired February 12, 2006.

6. *Comedians in Cars Getting Coffee*, "Dave Chappelle: Nobody Says 'I Wish I Had a Camera,'" season 10, episode 2, aired July 6, 2018 on Netflix.

7. Kute Blackson, "Episode 83: Laird Hamilton—How to Transform Fear and Find Your Flow," October 14, 2019, in *SoulTalk with Kute Blackson*, podcast, 1:03:46, http://podcast.kuteblackson.com/83-laird-hamilton-how-to-live-your-life-without-fear.

Chapter 4. The Miracle Zone

1. "Oprah Talks to Tyler Perry," O, *The Oprah Magazine*, December 2010.

2. Tyler Perry, *Higher Is Waiting* (New York: Spiegel & Grau, 2017).

3. Roger Brooks, "Tyler Perry's Hollywood: Diary of a Mad Black . . . Mogul," success.com, September 6, 2011; accessed September 10, 2020, https://www.success.com/tyler-perrys-hollywood-diary-of-a-mad-black-mogul/.

4. Ibid.

Chapter 5. You Were Made for More

1. *Oprah's SuperSoul Conversations*, "Malala Yousafzi: What is Your Defining Moment?," April 3, 2018, 31:29, https://omny.fm/shows/oprah-s-supersoul-conversations/malala-yousafzai-what-is-your-defining-moment.
2. Malala Yousafzai, *I Am Malala* (New York: Little, Brown, 2013), 255.

Chapter 6. The Ultimate Letting Go

1. Jeanne Marie Laskas, "The Mister Rogers No One Saw," *New York Times Magazine*, November 2, 2019.
2. Ibid.

Chapter 7. Unlocking the Magic

1. *Jiro Dreams of Sushi*, directed by David Gelb (2011).
2. "Fred Rogers Acceptance Speech—1997," YouTube, March 26, 2009; accessed September 10, 2020, https://www.youtube.com/watch?v=Upm9LnuCBUM.

ABOUT THE AUTHOR

For more than twenty years, Kute Blackson has been inspiring audiences around the world. Born in Ghana, West Africa, Kute's multicultural upbringing as the child of a Japanese mother and a Ghanaian father spanned four different continents. His unique lineage laid the foundation for his approach to breaking down barriers and unlocking an individual's true gifts and greatness. He is the author of *You Are the One* and hosts the podcast *SoulTalk with Kute Blackson*, but it is his charismatic videos and in-person teaching that has solidified his place as one of the next generation's leaders in personal development. *Inc.* magazine called him "the mindfulness guru billionaires go to for advice." Whether speaking at large-scale venues, working with clients one-on-one, helping organizations develop authentic leadership, or offering immersive transformational retreats around the world, Kute's electrifying approach and energy not only offer soul-stirring wisdom but ignite the heart and inspire courageous action.

Kute's mission is simple: to awaken and inspire people across the planet to access inner freedom, live authentically, and fulfill their true life's purpose.

Find out more: kuteblackson.com.